INFUSE

Activating Heaven on Earth

KEVIN BORDEAUX

Parsons Publishing House
Stafford, Virginia USA

INFUSE—Activating Heaven on Earth
by Kevin Bordeaux

Parsons Publishing House
P. O. Box 488
Stafford, VA 22554 USA
www.ParsonsPublishingHouse.com
Info@ParsonsPublishingHouse.com

Note: Disregarding English Grammar rules, Publishers have opted to reference satan and related names with lowercase letters.

ISBN-13: 978-1-60273-011-3
ISBN-10: 160273-0113
Library of Congress Control Number: 2014902791
Printed in the United States of America.
For World-Wide Distribution.

TABLE OF CONTENTS

DEDICATION

This book is dedicated to the four ladies who have believed in me and have been my biggest cheerleaders.

To my wife, Dianna, thank you for sacrificing so this book could be published.

To my mom, who is with Jesus, thank you for always being so proud of me. I remember you buying my first book in bulk and selling it out of your trunk.

To my grandmothers, Lovie and Mary Lou, you both forged a foundation of faith in my life. I am following Jesus today because you made Him a focus in your lives. Look forward to our reunion one day.

Finally, thank you God for redeeming me when I had nothing to offer.

FOREWORD

When Kevin asked me to write the foreword to his new book, I was honored. It is always a delight to a teacher to see a student applying what they have learned. Kevin was a student in the Southwestern Christian University Graduate School and has continually demonstrated compassion to take his expanding knowledge and apply it to reaching his generation for the Kingdom. The reading of this book will introduce you to the heartbeat of the author as well as the thinking of this generation. You will learn about both.

Kevin is a church planter enabling this searching generation to connect with a real God who is their Father. So this book is not esoteric, but practical, applying the lessons of the Kingdom to today's world. As you meditate on the Reflection Guides your passion will be stirred, and questioned, so you can connect better with a new generation. Old truths along with new ways are combined into a challenge for all. You will greatly benefit from the reading and applying this book to the world in your circle of influence.

Dr. Garnet E. Pike
Dean Emeritus, Southwestern Christian University (retired)
Master of Ministry Program

INTRODUCTION

"Our Father in heaven, may your name be kept holy. May your Kingdom come and may your will be done on earth as it is in heaven" (Matthew 6:9-10, NLT).

For centuries, the church has taught that the only purpose of salvation and the work of the cross is that we will go to heaven one day. "Saved" or "born again" are popular terms used by the Christian church to denote the totality of the gift of God in Christ.

Salvation has been limited to an event where a person prays a prayer and then has a special ticket to heaven. Christians indulge in Biblical end time teachings and books about the rapture. It seems as though the church is gazing up to heaven waiting for Christ to come and take us out of this hellish earth. The popular church songs are songs that help promote an "escapist" mentality. "I'll Fly Away" and "When We All Get to Heaven" saturate our Sunday morning worship services. Because of this mentality, the American church is dying while other religions are growing rapidly. This is because we have a utilitarian view of salvation. Salvation is a means to an end. It is merely a way to get eternal life insurance. For the Body of Christ to be awakened there must be a shift in the way we think; we must activate heaven on earth.

When Jesus' disciples asked Him to teach them how to pray, Jesus used nine lines to teach them about it. The opening of the prayer captures the heart of what God desires to happen in every believer's life: "Your Kingdom come and will be done on earth as it is in heaven." Jesus was stating that it is the Father's desire for heaven to come to earth. Will Christ return one day? Yes. But God's purpose of Christ's death on the cross was to provide mankind with a chance for heaven to invade earth. Salvation includes people redeemed to God in order to spend eternity with Him in heaven, but this is not the totality of salvation. God's desire is to have men and women in whom He can establish His Kingdom on earth.

The Kingdom of God has an "already/not yet" dialectic. We can experience some of the glory of the Kingdom now and share that with others, even though the total redemption of mankind and creation will come at the restoration of all things. The mentality of the church is shifting with this generation. This generation is not just teenagers, college-aged students, or young adults. The generation I am talking about is a nameless, faceless generation that is not bound or defined by age. They possess a desire like the Apostles and early church that want to invade and take hold of the present promise of God for their generation.

This generation, especially the younger generation, is an experiential generation. They invented the X-Games. Fifty years ago, the only people who jumped out of planes were the army; now, it is a weekend hobby for people. This generation does not look for a church based on a denominational affiliation; they look for the place where they can experience God's love and get involved in making an impact on their community. They couldn't care less who donated a pew, or whose grandpa built the steeple.

There is a present discontent in the church today, especially in the American church. People are tired of church, they are tired of continuing in bondage, and they are tired of just "waiting it out" to get to heaven. Their hearts are crying out for heaven to invade earth and for God's power to be present in their lives. As the Berlin Wall was decimated by hundreds of people who were tired of being in bondage, this generation is here to tear down the manmade traditions of the modern church that keeps it walled in and ineffective.

Infuse is about you connecting intimately with God and then helping others experience this in their daily life. The word "infuse" means, "to fill or pervade." The main thought of this book is simply for you to be infused with the presence of God, then live this out in addition to helping the world around you become infused with God's presence.

Imagine a dry sponge. Imagine your dirty dish caked with the nacho/chili dip you ate late last night. Your process may look like this: you grab the sponge, infuse it with water and soap, and then apply it to the dish for cleaning. We are the sponge. Heaven is the water main. Our relationship with God is the faucet. The world around us is the dirty dish. After you finish reading this book you should take what God is doing in you and spread it to the world around you.

CHAPTER 1

INFUSE AND INVADE

For God was in Christ, reconciling the world to himself, no longer counting people's sins against them. And He gave us this wonderful message of reconciliation. So we are Christ's ambassadors; God is making His appeal through us (2 Corinthians 5:19-20, NLT).

Jesus tells the Jewish leaders in John 5:19, "I tell you the truth, the Son can do nothing by himself. He does only what He sees the Father doing. Whatever the Father does, the Son does also" (NLT). Jesus was trying to explain to the religious leaders of that day that He was intimately connected to the Father and when He spoke, healed, or acted it was all because the Father prompted Him first. Jesus always acted with the authority of heaven. Jesus said, "The Son can do nothing by himself" (John 5:19).

Some Christians actually think that Jesus was some superhero who healed anybody anytime He wanted. This couldn't be further from the truth. Jesus never acted out of His own will. The Apostle John tells us that Jesus was sent from heaven in the Gospel of John chapter 1. God the Father gives His "seal of approval" by telling Jesus He was His beloved son and He was pleased with Him. Jesus came from another place, heaven, to this earth as an ambassador with heaven's authority and weight behind Him. He infused earth with heaven; He was the original "invader."

The decades of the 1950's-1970's brought us the sci-fi movies. Do you remember the cheesy alien movies of those decades? Earth lived in fear of these aliens invading earth and taking over earth. Those movies were littered with flying saucers, comical aliens, and humans who were afraid. They were afraid of the aliens from another planet taking over and infusing their culture into earth. Eventually the human race would be knocked out. In some of these movies you would have a representative alien who would talk to the human representative; it was much later before you met the head honcho of the aliens. They had an alien ambassador who would come to earth to talk and interact with the human leaders. This may be a far stretch for some, but this is our role as believers. We are from another world: heaven. We have been sent on behalf of our Head Honcho: Jesus. We are to invade earth and bring the culture of heaven to this earth. All Christians are all ambassadors.

To understand what Paul was saying in Second Corinthians 5:20, we must look at the role of ambassadors in that culture. When a country wanted to talk to another country about issues, they would send an ambassador. The ambassador was a diplomatic official sent from the throne room of the king with the king's orders and authority. The official would let the kingdom where he was going know what his king's desires and wishes were. Governments and kingdoms would shift their direction and actions based on this ambassador. The ambassador fully represented the government from where he was sent. The ambassador never spoke his own opinions or beliefs, but he spoke the king's decrees to the place where he was sent; he carried his kingdom's authority and power. The ambassador knew he was sent on a specific mission with the backing of his government.

Jesus was telling the Pharisees that He was sent by the King, as an ambassador, to this world in order that they may know the King's decrees. Jesus never spoke His own beliefs or opinions. When Jesus spoke, the situation changed around Him because He spoke with heaven's authority and heaven's power. He was infused and in tune with what was happening in heaven. He had a close relationship with the Father.

Once Jesus went to a pool at Bethesda and out of all the people there, He asked one particular man about being healed. Why didn't Jesus ask every person there? Jesus could do nothing by Himself alone. As an "invader," Jesus waited for what the Father wanted and infused earth with that.

Jesus heard the sound from heaven before He acted on earth. It started with a desire in heaven from God the Father and it was brought to earth through an ambassador: Jesus. God wants to bring heaven to earth, but He cannot do this as long as Christians are ignorant that they are heaven's ambassadors. What is God's will? No matter what situation you are in, God's will is to bring heaven to earth. No matter where you are or what you are doing, you can take that to the bank. Our goal in all situations is to be infused with heaven and then become an invader. This does not happen because we want it, but this will only happen when we are able to know what heaven is saying. There is a sound in heaven. When the sound of heaven invades earth, amazing things start to take place. Sound always precedes manifestation. So we have to be infused with the Bible daily and allow it to become real to us.

Before we will ever see God's transformation of the human heart on a major scale in our generation, we must know the sound of heaven. When Christians start reverberating the sound of heaven on earth through their lives, then we will see the results that the early church saw. The problem is that Christ-followers know what God **said**, but they have no idea what God is **saying** to them. Church folks adore the "historical" Jesus, but do not know Jesus personally. There is a desire that the Father has for your church, your community, and your life. In order to be an "invader," you must be in touch with heaven personally. You must be in a dynamic, real relationship with God. Before you allow this to happen, the Bible will be merely a text book and church will be a social club.

THE ROLE OF AN AMBASSADOR

Historically, an ambassador did three things: (1) he was in intimate relationship with the king, (2) he spoke on behalf of the king, and (3) he fully represented the kingdom from where he was sent.

1. Intimacy with the King

Intimacy with the King is the first requirement for an ambassador (who we can call an "invader"). The king would not take any old Joe off the street and send him on behalf of the kingdom; he would find someone who was in the throne room and knew his heart. The ambassador was well acquainted with the desire and wishes of the king; he was literally infused with the thoughts and intents of the king.

You must cultivate an intimate relationship with the King, who is Jesus. You must be in touch with His desires for your life, your church, and your city. This means that you must lead a life of personal worship. If you bypass His presence, He will bypass you as a qualified ambassador to fulfill His purposes. I am afraid that a lot of Christians and ministers know church, but they do not know Jesus. If Christians followed the Christ that is seen in the Bible, our lives and churches would look much different.

In my second year at Emmanuel College, I took a class called Biblical Interpretation. Dr. Michael Luper was teaching that class, and he was known as a tough professor, especially when it came to interpreting the Bible. He was an ex-tank driver—a man's man. Halfway through the semester, I turned in a paper that did not have a required sentence at the very end stating that I had followed every step thoughtfully and thoroughly. I did follow every step in that way, but because I did not have that statement, Dr. Luper marked out an "A" and put an "F" on it. He dropped our lowest grade, so in the long run it did not make much difference. At the end of class, He was asking for students' opinions on the class. I shared my thoughts about that paper and how I thought I was done wrong; I told him that it hurt my feelings, and I was offended. I will never forget his response: he paused with a concerned look on his face and said, "Well, I hate you feel that way. But, I have to look at Christ and I know that there were days that He hurt the disciples' feelings, like when He called Peter 'satan' and when He rebuked them."

He went on to say, "Our problem is we think Jesus was some sort of hippy who just walked around and patted people on the back. The truth is that we do not know the Christ of the Bible. He was a leader who had to hurt feelings all the time and did not get the approval of all the people." That statement hurt at first, but I had to really chew on it. I have come to the conclusion that a majority of Christ-followers do not know the Christ of the Bible. They simply know a Christ that their preacher, grandmother, or Sunday school teacher has taught them to believe.

It was Jesus who said in John chapter 15, "Abide in me and then you will be my disciples." Intimacy is not an option. I had a student ask me one time, "Can someone still go to heaven if they do not read the Bible, go to church, or pray?" They missed the point. Salvation is not primarily a golden ticket to Willy Wonka's Chocolate Factory, but it is a journey. God has commissioned us as ambassadors to our culture. In order to walk as ambassadors and be invaders, we must be in communion with our Heavenly Father and His people. When Paul said, "Take up the armor of God," he was literally saying, "Get militant about your relationship with God." The "armor of God" in Greek is a genitive of source. This means that the armor is sourced or found in God. We do not put the armor of God on as ambassadors because we can name all of it in the mornings as we pray. Paul was encouraging the Ephesians, who were in a highly spiritual evil culture, to "take up" or get militant about their relationship with God. The first key is intimacy. Before you can be an invader you have to be infused.

2. Speak on Behalf of the King

The second qualification for being an ambassador is speaking on behalf of the King. This is the part where you become the alien invader. Remember you have been born from above (heaven). Your citizenship is from there, not earth. This requires knowing what the King is saying. You cannot speak what you have never heard from God. A lot of leaders are great at being an echo, but there are very few that are a voice to their culture. John the Baptist was a voice crying in the wilderness. He spoke with heaven's government behind him. God is tired of earthly echoes; He wants people to hear the fresh Word from heaven for their culture.

What is God saying to you about your own life today? Jesus did not speak out of pity, frustration, emotion, or religion; Jesus spoke what heaven was already saying. God will not endorse what He never said. The Bible speaks volumes about our words and how we use them. Jesus said in Matthew 12:35-37, "A good person produces good things from the treasury of a good heart, and an evil person produces evil things from the treasury of an evil heart. And I tell you this, you must give an account on judgment day for every idle word you speak. The words you say will either acquit you or condemn you (NLT)." Proverbs 18:21 goes on to say, "The tongue can bring death or life" (NLT). When Jesus raised Lazarus from the dead, He did not go in and lay hands on him; He simply spoke. There is creative power behind the words we speak. We have the ability to speak life or speak death into situations. I believe that is why Paul states in First Corinthians chapter 14 that prophecy is more important than speaking in tongues. We should walk around prophesying (encouraging/exhorting) to one another and speaking life to others. We are bearers of the King's decrees. Once you have been infused, then you can infuse others.

3. Represent the Kingdom of God

The third requirement is that the ambassador fully represents his or her kingdom. This is the main part of the invader's role: you are God's representative on earth. Some people may never read the gospel, but they will read your life. Your job as a Kingdom Ambassador is to fully represent the Kingdom of God. Paul tells us that the Kingdom of God is righteousness, peace, and joy in the Holy Ghost (Romans 14:17). Church is membership, Sunday school, and board meetings, but the Kingdom goes outside the church. The world is hungry for these three qualities that Paul mentions. It is our job to be Jesus Christ to everyone with whom we come in contact. The world needs us to be infused with joy, peace, and understanding of our righteous standing with God through Christ.

The "invaders" are literally ambassadors for God's Kingdom. They are a generation who will carry the Kingdom of God into their jobs, homes, and schools. They know what God desires, and through their lives, they are able to bring heaven to earth. They recognize the sound of heaven and they resonate that sound on earth. They are infused and then invade.

THE INSTITUTIONAL CHURCH VS. THE LIVING ORGANISM

Many Christians have turned church into an organization or institution. They believe that you have certain actions at church meetings and other actions outside of church meetings. I remember a minister telling me one time that he was doing children's church and caught a young boy with a can of chewing tobacco, sometimes called dip. The young minister proceeded to tell the boy's father. The father carried the young boy aside and said, "Billy, I told you not to bring your dip to church. Do that at home!" The young boy was no more than eight years old. This illustration is a great example of the modern day church. We separate the sacred and secular. For some reason, the church has come to believe that some things should not be done in church, but they are acceptable outside of church.

We are the church. We, the Body of Christ, are a living organism that is designed to bring the life of Jesus wherever we go. Our homes, schools, and jobs should be our first church. When I was 22 years old, I was working at a concrete company; I had not yet accepted the call to full time ministry. One morning, I was walking up to the office and God spoke to me and said, "This is your church. You work with twelve men who are not saved; they are your congregation. Your sermon will be your life. These men will respond to Me based on how you conduct your life."

This radically changed the way I viewed my job. I stopped trying to get off work early to "go to church." Some people will gripe and complain when they are not able to do that. God spoke and said, "Your priority is not getting away from work to go to an institutional building; your priority should be living a holy life in front of these men so they will be saved." As invaders, our first duty is to carry the life of Jesus wherever we go. We are the church. We can carry the "church" anywhere we go.

I had a youth minister ask me one time about our form of evangelism for our ministry. He had concluded that each service should be "evangelistic," and for him, that meant preaching "leave your old way of life" every week. The principle behind that is, "Get them to church each week to get them saved." Invaders carry the life of Jesus into their world. I believe my specific purpose is to equip people to live out the Christian life with such conviction that the world around them becomes hungry for Jesus Christ. My dad is not a Christian. I could have become hurt and bitter, not because of him, but because of his associates. I was in my room one day and overheard a phone conversation where my dad was telling someone that one of his managers got frustrated and was cursing really bad. He went on to say how much of a Christian this guy claims to be and was laughing about the irony of this man's Christian profession. Believers, this is not the example we should be setting.

I saw this kind of behavior every day at work. There was one minister who borrowed money from many people and used his credibility as a minister to take advantage of people in this way. We had men showing up to our office threatening to beat him up if he did not repay them. People at work made jokes about him because of his lifestyle. There were other ministers who would look at women and make lewd jokes about them. When I approached them they would say things such as, "God knows we ain't perfect man, chill out."

That type of lifestyle does not make people hungry for the gospel. The more we die to ourselves, the more Jesus' life can be manifested through us. As ambassadors/invaders, we need to emit the fragrance of life into the world from our daily lives. It is what happens every day of our lives that makes the difference, not what happens in a service on a Sunday. We should make our homes sanctuaries for God's presence and for study of the Bible. Everyone who names the name of the Lord Jesus is a minister, or as Paul calls them, an ambassador.

In order for our lives to emit the presence of Christ everywhere we go, we must leave the old order of things. What I mean is that we must leave the mere formality of worship, prayer, Bible reading, and fellowship. We don't leave these things behind, but we allow the Spirit of God to breathe life on them. They become real to us through the Holy Spirit. This creates a "holy hunger." It is only when we are hungry for Christ that others become hungry. Believe me, they will not become hungry for formality; that is what they are running from. There needs to be a generation that rises up that is in touch with heaven. There needs to be a generation that rises up that knows what God is **saying**, not only what He **said**. We need a generation that doesn't view the Bible as a mere text book or instruction manual, but sweet manna. There needs to be a generation that comes forth who is hungry for the presence of the Father and will sacrifice everything to know Him.

Before we can invade and be ambassadors, carrying the King's heart to the world, we must be infused with heaven. Our lives must daily be permeated with a living, active relationship with our King.

REMEMBER THE EQUATION:

God's Word + God's Spirit + God's People = Infusion

REFLECTION GUIDE

Take some time to reflect on these questions:

What is one element you read from this chapter that challenged you? Why?

What do you need to change in your thinking to apply the principles from this chapter?

What did you have the most trouble receiving because of previous teachings? Why?

What did you like the most about this chapter? Why?

CHAPTER 2

INFUSED BY HIS VOICE

When the day of Pentecost came, they were all together in one place. Suddenly a sound like the blowing of a violent wind came from heaven and filled the whole house where they were sitting. They saw what seemed to be tongues of fire that separated and came to rest on each of them. All of them were filled with the Holy Spirit and began to speak in other tongues as the Spirit enabled them.

Now there were staying in Jerusalem God-fearing Jews from every nation under heaven. When they heard this sound, a crowd came together in bewilderment, because each one heard them speaking in his own language. Utterly amazed, they asked: "Are not all these men who are speaking Galileans? Then how is it that each of us hears them in his own native language? Parthians, Medes and Elamites; residents of Mesopotamia, Judea and Cappadocia, Pontus and Asia, Phrygia and Pamphylia, Egypt and the parts of Libya near Cyrene; visitors from Rome (both Jews and converts to Judaism); Cretans and Arabs—we hear them declaring the wonders of God in our own tongues!" Amazed and perplexed, they asked one another, "What does this mean?"

Some, however, made fun of them and said, "They have had too much wine."

Then Peter stood up with the Eleven, raised his voice and addressed the crowd: "Fellow Jews and all of you who live in Jerusalem, let me explain this to you; listen carefully to what I say. These men are not drunk, as you suppose. It's only nine in the morning! No, this is what was spoken by the prophet Joel:

"'In the last days, God says, I will pour out my Spirit on all people. Your sons and daughters will prophesy, your young men will see visions, your old men will dream dreams. Even on my servants, both men and women, I will pour out my Spirit in those days, and they will prophesy. I will show wonders in the heaven above and signs on the earth below, blood and fire and billows of smoke. The sun will be turned to darkness and the moon to blood before the coming of the great and glorious day of the Lord. And everyone who calls on the name of the Lord will be saved.'

"Fellow Israelites, listen to this: Jesus of Nazareth was a man accredited by God to you by miracles, wonders and signs, which God did among you through him, as you yourselves know. This man was handed over to you by God's deliberate plan and foreknowledge; and you, with the help of wicked men, put him to death by nailing him to the cross. But God raised him from the dead, freeing him from the agony of death, because it was impossible for death to keep its hold on him" (Acts 2:1-24).

THE START OF A NEW ERA

Since the day man sinned in the Garden of Eden, he has been confined to follow God through tradition, formality, and liturgical worship. They saw the miracles of God, received forgiveness through sacrifice, and participated in worship services, but until Acts chapter 2, God lived "outside" of His people. In Acts chapter 2, the new era began. You could say that Acts 2 was the actual end of the Old Covenant and beginning of the New Covenant. We see the earth and God's people infused with God's Spirit for the first time ever.

Peter's ancestors followed a literal cloud and a literal fire when they were wandering in the wilderness. Their worship was outward and was based on the sacrifice they offered. When Jesus Christ died on the cross, rose again and ascended to heaven, a new era began. No longer did the people of God worship based on their sacrifice; their worship was to the One who was the perfect sacrifice once and for all. They could not merely follow outwardly prescribed methods of worship; they now had to live by relationship, not by the Jewish regulations. This is the first time in history that the earth was infused with the Spirit of God. The Spirit of the Living God was not there to only manifest miracles and secure salvation, but to indwell human beings so they could live in a relationship with God.

THIS RELATIONSHIP IS DYNAMIC

Peter and the disciples watched Jesus Christ for over three years. They noticed that sometimes He would spit in a man's eyes to heal him while other times He just laid hands on the person. They probably wondered why He would walk up to a pool with hundreds of people who needed to be healed and only heal one person. It also probably sparked curiosity when He went off of the normal journey to go through Samaria. Jesus was a hard person to follow. I don't mean that it was hard with all the walking they did, but He was always doing something out of the ordinary. He broke down all the walls of the formality of religion. They also noticed that every day Jesus got up early in the morning to go pray, even before the sun came up.

This type of relationship is what it means to be a Christian. What puzzled Peter, James, and John about Jesus before the resurrection now made sense. They realized what it was to truly follow God instead of trying just to do religious work for Him. They experienced the "sound of heaven" in Acts 2. A whole new era for mankind came about. Men and women were no longer limited to outward liturgical worship services, but now they were called to a living, dynamic relationship with the Father through Jesus Christ. The liturgy now had meaning. Their Jewish festivals now had a real purpose. The Torah was alive to them.

We are able to know and find salvation through the finished work of Christ. This is the Christ that is recorded in history, primarily in the four Gospels. There are principles that Christ laid out in the Gospels: the "Be-attitudes" in Matthew chapter 5, for instance. There also are principles that were penned by the writers of the New Testament who were inspired by the Holy Spirit. Paul gives us some guidelines to follow in the Epistles, but the Bible is not primarily an instruction manual. The Bible is a living document; it breathes life to those who read it through the Holy Spirit.

Christians find it easy to obey prescribed rules of certain "do's" and "don'ts," but find it hard when the Bible does not speak about certain ways of life. For centuries, people have viewed the Bible as a history and a rule book. They know that it says to not do this or that, but it is the lowest form of relationship for a Christian to use the Bible as an instruction manual. There are many things to which the Bible does not directly speak; at times like that, we must follow our living relationship with Christ. God did not give us an instruction manual for us to follow. Following Christ does not mean saying a prayer of commitment and then believing a set of man-made rules. Following Christ does not mean only believing in a historic Christ who died and rose again. Following Christ is a day-by-day relationship where we are connected to Him and are listening to what He is speaking to us for that day; it is us living IN Him.

As the Israelites followed the cloud and fire, we are to follow the leading of the Holy Spirit on a daily basis. We must get up in the mornings asking God what He wants to speak to us. God does still speak, and it requires discipline to hear the sound of heaven. As ambassadors, we will never be able to bring heaven to earth if we do not know what God is saying to us specifically from heaven.

THE IMPORTANCE OF HEARING GOD'S VOICE

To some, this concept sounds flighty and a little over spiritual. I want to break down what it means to hear and usher in the sound of heaven in practical, down-to-earth terms. "Ushering in the Sound of Heaven" sounds really charismatic. It's not. It is simply knowing God and hearing God freshly on a daily basis. Isaiah 30:21 says, "Whether you turn to the right or left, your ears will hear a voice behind you saying, 'This is the way; walk in it.'" Isaiah goes on to say that they will turn from their idols and throw them away like a menstrual cloth. God was also telling the Israelites that He would send rain for their seed that they would sow in the ground. Later in the book it says:

> *This is what the Lord says—your Redeemer, the Holy One of Israel: "I am the Lord your God, who teaches you what is best for you, who directs you in the way you should go.* (Author's commentary: Now listen to this part of it) *If only you had paid attention to my commands, your peace would have been like a river, your righteousness like the waves of the sea" (Isaiah 48:17-18).*

As invaders, we must be infused. We are called to be in tune with the leading of the Lord. I would estimate that

90% of Christians never take time to intimately know what God is speaking to them. They live by their own opinions and ideals. They operate in their gifting and make leadership decisions, but never know what God is saying to them. When conflict arises they simply rely on intuition. When controversy arises they lean to their own understanding. Believers rarely take time to pause and hear what God is saying to them personally. I want to encourage you to evaluate your prayer life at this time. Are you occupied with worldly possessions and filling yourself on the things of the world, or are you occupied with the things of heaven?

As a young Christian, I came across Matthew 7:21 which opened my eyes. After reading this Scripture, I came to the realization that many religious people, or may I say religious Christians (which is an oxymoron), will not enter the Kingdom of God. Again, Christianity does not mean believing a set of prescribed principles and laws. The essence of the Christian life is passionately and intimately following after the heart of the Father. Anything less than that is unacceptable to God. Matthew 7:21-23 says:

> *"Not everyone who says to me, 'Lord, Lord,' will enter the kingdom of heaven, but only the one who does the will of my Father who is in heaven. Many will say to me on that day, 'Lord, Lord did we not prophesy in your name, and in your name drive out demons and in your name perform many miracles?' Then I will tell them plainly, 'I never knew you. Away from me, you evildoers!'"*

I have heard people say that this refers to non-Christian people. The word "knew" in this passage can be compared to the same word the King James Version uses in Genesis to describe Adam and Eve's intimate relationship in the garden of Eden. What Jesus was saying was, "I never had a true relationship with you. You worked hard at the church.

You built your own kingdom. You believed in Me mentally, but you never took time to know Me intimately."

Just attending a church service or doing work for the church is not what God desires primarily. It takes sacrifice to hear and heed the voice of the Father. I want to give you an outline of some ways to structure your life to gain this intimate relationship with Him.

HOW TO HEAR THE SOUND OF HEAVEN

God is waiting to speak to you. This may scare you. You may be asking, "What does it mean that God speaks? What does He sound like? How can I distinguish from His voice, my voice, and the voice of satan?" Let me just say for the record: I have never heard God's audible voice. Maybe I am not that spiritual. I have never seen angels or demons, either. So, this levels the playing field. We can all hear God speaking to our hearts.

In a message on prayer, Pastor Erwin McManus told the story of his son Aaron. He started by saying that he was not going to convict the people to pray more or harder for every religion prays hard. His central theme was that we are the only religion that is able to hear the voice of God and respond to it. His son Aaron was struggling with the idea of "hearing God." He told Erwin that he had never heard the voice of God. His dad simply told him that when God speaks he will know. A couple of months later Erwin McManus sent Aaron to a Christian camp where a bully talked trash and said something to Aaron about his mom. Aaron, as Erwin explains, was a pretty laid back kid, but he got really mad and threatened to hurt the boy. Camp counselors got involved and called Erwin, so he went down to the camp and talked to Aaron. His son was still really mad and upset, and he refused to apologize and forgive the other boy. Erwin McManus asked his son, "Son, what is God telling you to do?" Aaron, without thinking said, "To forgive him." McManus went ballistic and said, "Aaron, Aaron, do you know what just happened?" Aaron was confused and said no. Erwin screamed with excitement, "You just heard God!"[1] This is a great example of how easy it is to hear the voice of God, and how easy it is to miss the voice of God. Dr. G. Earl Beatty said in a ministry class while I was attending Emmanuel College, "You can hear God in everything, but miss Him in anything."

God desires for you to walk in blessing. Your desire should be to complete the will of the Father for your life. This means that you will have to structure your private life to hear the voice of God. A number of Christians have the Martha mentality of serving and working, but we find very few that want to sit at Jesus' feet and listen to His words. This is how you hear the sound of heaven:

1. Your Position

When you accept Christ as your Savior, you are a child of God. You are positioned as a son or daughter of God. You cannot work for more of God's love or grace; He fully accepts you. This is the first step in developing intimacy with God. Many people view their heavenly Father the way they view their earthly father and think He will treat them the same way their earthly father treats them. It takes years for some people to understand the unsearchable riches of God's love and grace.

I was once told that, as Christians, we have a standing and a state. Our standing is perfect in God's sight; we cannot earn the grace of God. Ephesians 2:8 says, "For it is by grace you have been saved, through faith—and this is not from yourselves, it is the gift of God." Our faith in the finished work of Christ on the cross is what allows us to access salvation. Our standing is much different from our state. We are still living in this world and in this flesh; there is a battle going on. Our state is imperfect. Our current state is that we are still living in a fallen world and in rotting flesh. There are shortcomings and problems that we have. Because of this, we must posture ourselves to be touched by God and hear His voice daily.

2. Your Posture

> *The LORD appeared to Abraham near the great trees of Mamre while he was sitting at the entrance to his tent in the heat of the day. Abraham looked up and saw three men standing nearby. When he saw them, he hurried from the entrance of his tent to meet them and bowed low to the ground. He said, "If I have found favor in your eyes, my lord, do not pass your servant by. Let a little water be brought, and then you may all wash your feet and rest under this tree. Let me get you something to eat, so you can be refreshed and then go on your way—now that you have come to your servant" (Genesis 18:1-5).*

Abraham was visited by God. The three men represent what theologians call a "theophany." The Lord used these three men to actually reveal who He was to Abraham. In response, Abraham physically bowed down and then served them. How many times has God shown up in our lives when we were expecting to be served? Abraham overcame pride and postured himself before God. The Lord's response to this is seen later when He spoke to him about his destiny. Abraham positioned himself to hear God's voice by humbling himself and serving others.

In order to posture yourself to hear the voice of God, you must first be willing to put yourself in a place to hear. The first thing Abraham did was change his posture when God came to meet with him. Spending quality time in the Word of God is a way of posturing yourself before Him. He never speaks apart from His Word. Take your Bible and a notebook and find a quiet place away from everything. I had a Bible professor once tell me that we should make appointments with God. If your schedule allows, this is a great way to posture yourself to hear His voice.

The next thing to do is go through a certain book of the Bible. If you are a new Christian, stay with the New Testament when you seek to hear the voice of God. When you read the Old Testament, get a good understanding of the culture and context of the book you are reading or you may end up with some crazy doctrines.

Here is a method I learned from Pastor Wayne Cordero that he shared at Exponential Conference in Orlando, Florida when he spoke on healthy leadership.[2] It is called the S.O.A.P Method. You start by going systematically through a book in the Bible. Let's start with Matthew. You will break down the Bible according to thought. Now, many Bibles are broken down that way.

This is the S part called, "SCRIPTURE." What is the Scripture you are studying? The next is called "OBSERVATION." You take time to observe what the writer is saying to his audience, and not to you, per se. Write down who he is speaking to, what is being said, and the tone of the passage. This is the context of their culture. Then you move to "APPLICATION." Write down how this applies to your life specifically. Christians want God to speak to them about direction for their life, but they will not allow God to speak to them about shaping their character. God is more concerned with speaking to who you are than what you do. Hearing the voice of God is a time when God is allowed to shape you and mold you. The goal of every Christian is "Christ formed in you." This is the application part. What is the Holy Spirit dealing with you specifically? How is He shaping your life? The final part is "PRAYER." Write down a short prayer describing what you are asking God to do in light of what He has shown you.

Here is an example from my life:

August 30th

Scripture:
Matthew 1:1-17 (genealogy)

Observation:

Matthew uses Abraham and David when he opens up. He does this for two reasons. The first reason is because He wanted to teach them that Jesus is first, the covenant promise and fulfillment of the never-ending throne of David. He is the promised Messiah to the Israelites. Secondly, he uses Abraham to show that Jesus is also the savior to the Gentiles. He breaks it down from universalism and particularism. He also uses five women throughout the genealogy. These are not women of rapport. They have bad histories and were failures, but God used them.

Application:

Every one of these people listed in the genealogy all believed God at His Word. They trusted that God would fulfill the Abrahamic Covenant and the Davidic Covenant. They lived their lives to the fullest, knowing that they played a part in the fulfillment of God's Plan. The Holy Spirit began to impress on my heart that I should move from a lifetime perspective to a generational perspective. If I will believe by faith and step out, then I will place a rung on the ladder. When I leave earth someone else can step on it, and then they can place a rung on the ladder so someone else can step up.

As I am writing this, Jason Upton is singing, "Every Word that is sent down from heaven will not return until it has succeeded what it is meant to do."

Prayer:

Lord, help me to have a generational perspective. Thank you for leading Matthew to inspire us from his genealogy. Thank you that you are not just doing something in me, but through me where people who have not been born yet will use my life to go to new and higher levels. THANK YOU!! Amen.

3. Your Perseverance

Hearing and responding to God is a discipline that will take perseverance because there are many things that come to take our time and energy. This type of teaching sounds great while you are reading it, but it is when the craziness of life comes that this is most important to put into practice. The time of crisis is not the time to try to start hearing the voice of God. It is imperative for believers to learn this discipline before they face great tests.

The Alaskan Bull Moose begins eating and fattening up in the summer. The reason they do this is because the fall of the year is when they mate and fight with other male moose. It is the heaviest moose that wins because they are able to throw their weight and break the antlers of the other moose.[3] This is a great illustration of what it means to hear and respond to the voice of God. It is better to prepare and prevent than repair and repent.

My life is most miserable when I am not focusing on the leading of the Holy Spirit. I have found myself questioning decisions and having doubts about the future when I have not taken quality time to listen to God. One of the great plans of our enemy, satan, is to get us so busy that we live by religious principles and not by the personal leading of the Holy Spirit.

I wish I could tell you that every time you take time with God, there is an aura in the room and you can feel His presence. The truth of the matter is, however, that most of the time you will question whether or not God is speaking to you. God uses dry times and seasons to see if we will persevere to grow deeper with Him, or if we will withdraw back to our old lifestyles. We cannot pursue God and worship based on what type of feeling we get. My driest times with God have been my richest times with God.

There was an old Chinese farmer who grew trees; he was part of a village of tree farmers. During the spring time of the year, other farmers gave extra water to try and help their trees grow. The old Chinese farmer did not give any extra water and at times it looked like he had starved the trees. The other farmers did not understand it. A drought came to the land and the other farmer's trees died, but the old Chinese farmer's trees flourished. His trees learned to tap deep down into the water under them; their roots grew deeper.[4]

Seeking God takes perseverance. Sometimes God will withdraw His manifest presence so we will learn to grow deeper in Him. He wants us to love Him, not lust after a feeling.

4. Your Priority

God's presence must be your priority. You will find out what is important to people when you look at the management of their time. Time is the only resource we can never get back once we lose it. Time in the presence of God is never time wasted. For someone to bring heaven to earth, he or she must be a person of the presence. One of the ways to prepare your heart to receive from God is to worship. It seems that all Christians pray at some level, but never spend time in intimate worship with God in their private life. My spiritual walk with God grew leaps and bounds when I took time to worship God and enjoy His presence. We should be very thankful that a God so holy would love us enough to want to commune with us.

I once knew a man who had a specific prayer time. Each night, this gentleman had an appointment with God at the same time. If you were at the house at this time, you would have to wait an hour before he got back from his prayer time. I have found that it is best for me to spend time with God before my day begins. I say this for a couple of reasons. First, if you wait until the end of the day, you will find that the day has taken your time and energy, and there is no time left for God. The second reason is that you will need God's wisdom and understanding in order to deal with the issues of the day. You may feel the Holy Spirit prepare you for coming trials or circumstances.

I will never forget one morning while I was praying, God said, "Glorify me in everything that comes your way today." I thought, "God, can you give me something better than that?" I was playing basketball with some of the guys at school and one guy started taunting me and I said some smart aleck comments to him. I immediately realized that I had failed the Lord. I also realized that I need to listen carefully everyday to Him. This has helped me make His voice a priority in my life. Let's allow God to infuse us with His Word and His will so we can invade earth with His love.

CONCLUDING THOUGHTS

The sound of heaven in Acts 2 was the sound of a mighty rushing wind. At that moment, mankind was changed forever. Heaven came to earth. An invader is someone who is able to discern the voice of God and respond to His voice. They recently found that the Sequoia trees in Yosemite National Park were falling to the ground because their root system was being trampled. The park had to put sacred enclosures around the root system to protect the trees. The enemy's plan for our lives is to trample our root system. We must put up sacred enclosures in our lives to protect our time to hear the voice of God.

Jesus was preoccupied with being infused by God's presence and plan. Because He was infused with hearing God, He was able to be the prototype invader.

End Notes:

[1] McManus, Erwin. "Hearing God." Catalyst Conference. Gwinnett Conference Center, Atlanta. Thursday Oct. 2007. Lecture.

[2] Cordero, Wayne. "Healthy Leadership." Exponential Conference. First Baptist of Orlando, Orlando. Spring 2006. Lecture.

[3] Larson, Craig. "Spiritual Warfare." SermonIllustrations.com December 2001.

[4] Cordero, Wayne. "Healthy Leadership." Exponential Conference 2006. Orlando, FL.

REFLECTION GUIDE

Take some time to reflect on these questions:

What is one element you read from this chapter that challenged you? Why?

What do you need to change in your thinking to apply the principles from this chapter?

What did you have the most trouble receiving because of previous teachings? Why?

What did you like the most about this chapter? Why?

CHAPTER 3

INFUSED WITH INTIMACY

After this I looked, and there before me was a door standing open in heaven. And the voice I had first heard speaking to me like a trumpet said, "Come up here, and I will show you what must take place after this." At once I was in the Spirit, and there before me was a throne in heaven with someone sitting on it. And the one who sat there had the appearance of jasper and ruby. A rainbow that shown like an emerald, encircled the throne. Surrounding the throne were twenty-four other thrones, and seated on them were twenty-four elders. They were dressed in white and had crowns of gold on their heads. From the throne came flashes of lightning, rumblings and peals of thunder. In front of the throne, seven lamps were blazing. These are the seven spirits of God. Also in front of the throne there was what looked like a sea of glass, clear as crystal. In the center, around the throne, were four living creatures, and they were covered with eyes, in front and in back. The first living creature was like a lion, the second was like an ox, the third had a face like a man, the fourth was like a flying eagle. Each of the four living creatures had six wings and was covered with eyes all around, even under its wings. Day and night they never stop saying:

"Holy, holy, holy
is the Lord God Almighty,

who was, and is, and is to come."
Whenever the living creatures give glory, honor and thanks to him who sits on the throne and who lives for ever and ever, the twenty-four elders fall down before him who sits on the throne, and worship him who lives for ever and ever. They lay their crowns before the throne and say:
"You are worthy, our Lord and God,
to receive glory and honor and power,
for you created all things,
and by your will they were created
and have their being." (Revelation 4:1-11).

THE WORSHIP WAR

One of the primary battles that churches in the past few decades face is the battle over worship styles. The world has changed rapidly since the early to mid 1900s, but the church has stayed the same. This is true of the style of buildings, dress codes, aesthetics, and music in the church. The world looks at the church as "behind the times." Today's generation has the idea about God and the church that it worked for grandma and grandpa, but it is irrelevant to me.

Think about it. People go to a building that looks like no other building and seems irrelevant. They sit in a piece of furniture that is used nowhere else, (church pew) which also seems irrelevant. They hear songs that seem like they are from the 1600s, and that also adds to the irrelevance. Finally, a pastor tells them that this ancient book is relevant to their lives. How do we show the world that God is relevant?

There are two things that unlock the key to someone's heart: laughter and music. We hold a special reverence for those who make us laugh, and we also hold a special place in our hearts for music. There has been a great war over music in the church. Some churches have tried doing one service for the younger generation and one service for the older generation. There is a story behind what I am writing. I had not been to church in years, but I was saved at the age of 20. I saw the church I was saved in fight over worship; it was a bloodbath. Staff cycled in and out. People took sides. It was a sad time in the Kingdom. I write this simply to share my experience with you because I have been a wounded soldier in this war.

Another experience I had was when I was working in a youth ministry at a different church six years later where we saw the power of God poured out in people's lives. The church quickly became multi-cultural and lives were changed on a weekly basis. As a youth pastor, I had the privilege of seeing teenager's lives changed because of heart-felt worship.

Whatever the style of music, a church must be careful of losing their sense of awe while singing unto God. I see some of the younger generation look down upon hymns. They don't understand the power behind those songs. I personally love the hymns of the church which have powerful stories and in-depth theology. But I also see the older generation sit down and not sing at all during the contemporary worship. There is a heart issue on both sides. Singing unlocks something inside of us. Singing unto God is a form of obedience. There is a good reason why there are so many worship wars. One church can use worship to divide a congregation where another church uses it to draw people into God's Kingdom.

THE BATTLE OF INFUSION

God inhabits the praise of His people and God is omnipresent. He is everywhere at once, He never leaves us, and He shows up in "thick" portions in some places. It's a strange thing, but it's a fact. You will never see God go where He is not welcomed by His people. The problem lies in the fact that satan does not want God's presence and God's people to interact.

When God's presence pours into people's lives their lives are changed forever. Drug addictions are broken, pornography cannot be a stronghold any longer, and other bondages are stripped from an individual. It is not a battle for style, it is a battle for the presence of God. The idea is not what style of music you do or for how long you do it. The key to unlocking the "sound of worship" as an invader is personally welcoming and honoring God's presence in our lives. Now, I find myself more in worship thanking God for His Holy Spirit in me, His presence in our gathering and His power that is available instead of begging God to come. He is here. His power is available to all. Our problem is that either we are totally unaware or so emotionally bogged down that we don't enjoy His presence.

The key to being an invader is being infused. Revelation 4 is a perfect picture of what is going on in heaven. This is the ultimate worship service! There is an awesome light show with loud thunder and lightning. People are seeking God 24 hours a day, falling at His feet, and crying out, "Holy, holy, holy." If worship is a small part of your life you will not like heaven's worship. There is extreme worship going on in heaven. Take a moment and read Revelation chapter 4 again. Reflect in silence on what you think that would look and sound like. For us to experience the power of heaven on earth, we must look at the type of worship that is going on in heaven.

THE WORSHIP OF HEAVEN

Revelation 4 gives us a great illustration of heavenly worship. Some things must be in place no matter what style you choose to do. There is a process to worship as heaven worships. I want us to take a few minutes to see this process.

1. Heavenly Worship is Spiritual in Nature.

"At once I was in the Spirit..." (Revelation 4:2).

Heavenly worship requires, first of all, that we view worship as a spiritual experience and connection with God. John, the writer of Revelation, records that he was "in the Spirit." Some people believe that "in the Spirit" is where your eyes roll in the back of your head and you chant for hours. John simply was connecting with God.

So many times we put emphasis on the right song or style of worship. Some people believe they have to feel right or be perfect before they can enter into spiritual worship. Worship is an attitude of the heart. Spiritual worship is not goose bumps; I get goose bumps at really good movies. Spiritual worship is when your whole focus is on the greatness of who God is and your condition of grace before Him. Spiritual worship does not happen when you come to God with heavy burdens, and they are all you can think about. Spiritual worship does not happen with your arms folded, sitting down, and thinking about how ready you are to be home after the service. Spiritual worship requires that you give your undivided attention to God. It requires that you focus on His position on the throne. It requires a thankful heart for being redeemed. It requires a place of gratitude for a holy, transcendent God that has chosen you.

2. God is Recognized as the One on the Throne.

> *...and there before me was a throne in heaven with someone sitting on it. And the one who sat there had the appearance of jasper and ruby. A rainbow that shown like an emerald, encircled the throne. (Revelation 4:2b-3).*

This may seem weird, but God is the One on the throne, not you. So many times we come to have a spiritual worship experience with God, and we use our mind, will, emotions, and intellect to focus on ourselves and problems. In Pentecostal/Charismatic circles, worship is getting a good feeling and you can even end up worshipping feelings, instead of God.

Heavenly worship not only requires that you position yourself, but also requires that you find the right posture. I have heard it said again and again that worship is your response to who God is. In Revelation, John sees God as the One on the Throne. He loses the sense of where he is and what he is facing because he sees God on the throne. The Apostle John is on an island; he is old and weak. John did not pour out his problems to Jesus when He appeared to him; he was focused on His majesty. I love what happens after Jesus shows up: they start talking about the state of the church in John's generation.

This is so important when worshiping. Sometimes you need to just stop and recognize that He is working all things out for His pleasure. He did not make the bad things happen, but you can be confident that He will use them for His glory and your benefit. If God is who He says He is, then He requires a lot more response from us. We should get lost in Him because He is on the throne; the One on the Throne deserves a great response. The response is not in how high you jump or if you wave your hands while they are lifted. The right response is when you become overwhelmed with the majesty, greatness, and glory of the King.

3. Heavenly Worship always has Expression Toward God.

> *Whenever the living creatures give glory, honor and thanks to him who sits on the throne and who lives*

> *for ever and ever, the twenty-four elders fall down before him who sits on the throne, and worship him who lives for ever and ever. They lay their crowns before the throne and say: (Revelation 4:9-10).*

Worship that ushers in heaven to earth is always expressive in some manner. Please read this IMPORTANT disclaimer: Everyone will express it differently! Don't make people express worship like you do. I am not an overly expressive person. I am pretty reserved; however, I do express my gratitude and thankfulness to God in worship. I really don't enjoy jumping or acting crazy. Have I done it? Yes. Is it wrong? No. I have a friend who is wild, and he looks like a wild man during worship. He loves God and expresses His love that way to God. The key is not judging the expression, but rather allowing God to judge the heart of the expression. The expression of love looks different in all relationships.

If you love someone, you will express your love for that person. My wife knows I love her because I express love. It grieves me to see worship at a church that does not encourage people to express their love for God at all. When you learn to express your love for God in worship, then you will learn to express it in every aspect of your life. The elders around the throne fell down before Him, laid their crowns down, and said (or sang) to God. They prostrated themselves on the ground before God. They laid their crowns down before Him. A crown denotes your position and honor. The elders laid down their glory, pride, and accomplishments. They also "said" unto God. They spoke words of blessing and honor over God. Heavenly worship is expressive. The elders expressed their love and devotion to God by saying. They used words to speak out loud to the Lord and express their love to Him. Some Christians don't have any response or expression in worship.

KEYS TO UNLOCKING HEAVENLY WORSHIP

> *Therefore, I urge you, brothers, in view of God's mercy, to offer your bodies as a living sacrifices, holy and pleasing to God—this is your true and proper worship. Do not conform any longer to the pattern of this world, but be transformed by the renewing of your mind. Then you will be able to test and approve what God's will is—his good, pleasing and perfect will (Romans 12:1-2).*

This passage of Scripture in Romans sums up the true meaning of worship. Notice that Paul does not mention styles, for styles will change. Paul does not mention a certain hymn or chorus. Paul urges the Romans to offer their lives unto God. He goes on to say that this is true worship. Spiritual worship is a lifestyle that reflects God's mercy to the individual and a transformed life by His grace. God does not want us to just sing to Him or about Him on Sunday morning, but God wants us to reflect His glory at our jobs, homes, and schools. He wants us to be infused and then invade. We find it easy to sing about God's love, but cannot show God's love in a practical way. When the lady at McDonald's messes up our order, we must show the love we just sang about one hour ago. God's desire is that His love and grace fill the earth, and we are the vessels for that.

1. God wants ALL of you.

Paul tells the Romans to offer up their bodies as a spiritual act of worship. There were some heretical sects that declared we could sin with our bodies and be holy because our spirits are holy. Prostitution was an act of worship in that culture. Some of the early Christians who were converted kept on doing things that they had been doing. Being saved to them was a license to sin. However, Paul urged the Romans to offer up their bodies as a sacrifice to God.

We have the same problem nearly 2,000 years later. Christians have been taught that you can mentally believe in Jesus, pray to Him, and be saved. This is especially true in America where we have an idolatrous culture. Our understanding of worship is what happens only on Sunday mornings. Years ago I was praying with a good friend before our youth service, and he shared what God shared with him. He said, "The service does not start when we get here, the service starts when we leave. When we show up on Wednesdays, it should be an overflow of our worship all week long. God will not give us on Wednesdays that which we will not seek for the rest of the week."

We live in the days of grace. I thank God for our understanding of God's grace through the finished work of the cross. We must be careful not to cheapen the grace that was lavished on us. Our prayer cannot be, "Your kingdom come..." when our lifestyles speak, "our will be done." God's Kingdom cannot be established where human will is on the throne. We watch what we want to, we listen to what we want to, our bodies are ours, our thoughts are ours, and the kingdom we are establishing is ours. It is time for us to repent before God and let Him know that we want His Kingdom to come, and that we want to give up our wills to Him. For our world, and especially our nation, to see the glory of God come, we must allow our whole lives to be set apart for Him. That is true worship.

God spoke to me about this a few years ago before I accepted the full-time call to ministry. I was praying one night and God said, "You have set Me apart for your purposes, now is the time when I will set you apart for My purposes." I knew at that moment it would take great submission on my part to follow the Lord. I agreed with the will of God, but I did not submit to the will of God. There is a big difference between submitting to the will of God and agreeing with it. As long as the will of God goes where you want it to, and does what you want it to do, you will follow it. Submitting to the will of God means that you will submit even when you do not like it and do not agree with it. The point is that God wants all of you.

2. Respond to God's Revelation.

Paul shares this phrase with the Romans, "in view of God's mercy, offer..." (Romans 12:1). Essentially, Paul was saying, "Because of who God is to you and what He has done, present yourself in a worshipful lifestyle to God." Worship is simply responding to the revelation of God. Throughout the Bible, people responded to God revealing Himself to them. Moses took off his shoes at the burning bush and received God's orders for his life. Abraham left everything when God revealed Himself. Paul committed himself to serving Christ when he encountered Him on the Damascus Road.

We can only worship what we know of God. Christ-followers who don't have a revelation of Him and the finished work of the cross find it hard to live a lifestyle of worship. God is seeking those who want to know Him, but He will not reveal Himself to those who do not truly care. As a Christian, it is vitally important to pray and ask God to reveal Himself to you. In the book of Ephesians 1:17-20, Paul prays for the church at Ephesus. This prayer can give us insight into what the Apostle Paul considered important for believers.

> *I keep asking that the God of our Lord Jesus Christ, the glorious Father, may give you the Spirit of wisdom and revelation, so that you may know him better. I pray also that the eyes of your heart may be enlightened in order that you may know the hope to which he has called you, the riches of his glorious inheritance in his holy people, and his incomparably great power for us who believe. That power is the same as the mighty strength he exerted when he*

raised Christ from the dead and seated him at his right hand in the heavenly realms. (Ephesians 1:17-21).

I pray every day for the "spirit of wisdom and revelation" in order to know God better. For a believer to unlock heavenly worship, he or she has to know who God is. There are many benefits we have in knowing Christ, but so often believers live an impoverished lifestyle because they really don't know who God is. The identity of who we are is ultimately locked up in the knowledge of who He is. Paul tells the Ephesians that they have a calling, an inheritance, and the power of God available to them by having the eyes of their heart opened. It excites me to know that there is a specific calling on my life, an inheritance to help me fulfill that calling, and the power of God working in me.

Some people wonder why I have such joy and peace in my life. It is because I know who God is and that there is a calling on my life. Our lives can come into perspective when we realize that we have an assignment from God and that He has empowered us to fulfill that assignment. The key to giving your life over to Him in worship is having God reveal Himself to you. You will probably ask, "What is my calling and assignment?" The calling and assignment is responding to God no matter the cost.

3. Expression is a Fruit of Worship.

This passage in Romans tells us to "offer or present" our lives to God. A true offering requires expression to God. God's anointing will not manifest in those who are not hungry for His presence. When you find people hungry for God's presence you will find people who are expressive in some way. This can mean for one person that their head is bowed, and they are thanking God for His redeeming work. Another person may kneel. Others may raise their hands.

The act of expression is not as important as what ignites that expression. If a charismatic worship leader ignites your expression then you are responding to him/her. The igniting of our expression should be because we love God and are grateful for what He has done.

I express love to people, and that is how they know that I love them. The reason I have friends is because I express my love to them. They want to be in my presence because I express my love to them. Some people wonder why they cannot "feel" the presence of God. It is because their worship does not focus on God. You can tell a lot by body language. I can tell by their body language when someone really wants to hear what I have to say, and when they really don't care. I believe God is the same way. He can tell who really wants to be around Him and who is indifferent.

Paul shares his heart with his protégé, Timothy, in his 1st letter to him. 1 Timothy 2:8 says, "I want men everywhere to lift up holy hands in prayer, without anger or disputing." The Apostle Paul's desire is that people everywhere lift up holy hands. This can be taken as symbolic or literal. I like to look at it both ways. Paul did not want only expressive worship, but holy expressive worship. He wanted young Timothy to encourage his people to express their love to God by an expression of holiness. Whether the lifting of the hands was literal or symbolic there was still an expression.

The Hebrew culture viewed lifting hands as a sign of recognizing God's blessing on them. They wanted God's blessing and recognized it. It was customary for the early Christians to lift up their palms to heaven as a sign for help. I know that I need God and need His help. I don't lift up my hands because of my denomination; I lift my hands because I want God to know that I love Him and need Him.

4. Our Home is the First Worship Sanctuary.

The reason people do not worship at church is because they do not worship at home. If they do not lift up their hands and cry out at church, it is because they do not do it at home. This is the one point that I feel most strongly about. My life was radically transformed when I started worshipping at home. There was an extra room in my mom and dad's house, so each night I would retreat there and seek God's face. I can still remember when I first began to feel the presence of the Holy Spirit. I hungered for my meeting with God each night. It was out of my personal worship experience that I began to enter into and enjoy corporate worship.

We must remember that the battle is for the presence. Worship invites God's presence into a place. When you worship at home you invite the presence of God into your home. As Christians, a lot of us invite everything and anything into our homes, but never spend time inviting the presence of God. These same people wonder why their children act like the devil. If heaven is to invade earth, we must be people who have personal worship. I urge you as you read this book to find a personal place to connect with God, put a worship CD on, and express your gratitude to God. Our churches will be changed forever when we make our homes the first church.

CONCLUDING THOUGHTS

Here is the point: if we are going to see the glory of heaven invade earth, we must be people who are passionately in love with God. God desires radical worshippers in the earth. You will never find a Scripture in the Bible that tells people not to be expressive. The Psalms are full of expressive praise and thanksgiving to God. The Hebrew culture was one of celebration, dancing and joy. If we have grace, then why are we often so apathetic?

Closing thought: Jesus never condemned anyone for being emotionally passionate for Him, but He did condemn those who were emotionally dry and apathetic toward Him.

REFLECTION GUIDE

Take some time to reflect on these questions:

What is one element you read from this chapter that challenged you? Why?

What do you need to change in your thinking to apply the principles from this chapter?

What did you have the most trouble receiving because of previous teachings? Why?

What did you like the most about this chapter? Why?

CHAPTER 4

INFUSED WITH WARFARE

Then war broke out in heaven. Michael and his angels fought against the dragon, and the dragon and his angels fought back. But he was not strong enough, and they lost their place in heaven. The great dragon was hurled down—that ancient serpent called the devil, or Satan, who leads the whole world astray. He was hurled to the earth, and his angels with him.

Then I heard a loud voice in heaven say:
"Now have come the salvation and the power and the kingdom of our God, and the authority of his Messiah. For the accuser of our brothers and sisters, who accuses them before our God day and night, has been hurled down. They triumphed over him by the blood of the Lamb and by the word of their testimony; they did not love their lives so much as to shrink from death. Therefore rejoice, you heavens and you who dwell in them! But woe to the earth and the sea, because the devil has gone down to you! He is filled with fury, because he knows that his time is short" (Revelation 12:7-12).

REAL WAR WITH REAL ENEMIES

There was a pastor whom we will call Steve. Steve was on an airplane one day when he noticed that the man next to him was mumbling or sort of praying. The pastor leaned over and told the man, "I believe in prayer, too." The man responded by saying, "Sir, I don't think you understand; I am on an assignment. I am praying for the downfall of pastors across America."[5]

When you look at the book of Revelation we see that there is another sound going on in heaven right now; it is the sound of war. It is true that some Christians are more wrapped up in the war of the Middle East than they are in the war of the heavens. Satan has brought an all out assault against the children of God. He knows that his time is short, so he is calling all reserves. While Christians hold on—singing their sweet little hymns and waiting for Jesus to come back—the enemy of our souls has launched his army. This is a real war with a real enemy.

This generation faces more opposition and deception than any other generation on the face of the earth. The modern Christian goes to church, sings church songs, and says church things.These attacks will not be stopped by smarter Christians who know more apologetics, but the attacks require Christians who are aware and engage in this spiritual war.

There is more sin and corruption in this generation than in generations past, but we need to realize that God has entrusted us with overcoming this corruption and setting a standard. We must remember, "Where sin abounds grace does much more abound" (Romans 5:20, *paraphrased*). But this will not and cannot happen until Christians engage in warfare. There may be millions of Christians standing and gazing up into heaven waiting for Jesus to come back (like the boys in Acts 1), but there is a remnant that wants to charge the gates of hell and let the enemy know that we will be victorious.

For our struggle is not against flesh and blood, but against the rulers, against the authorities, against the powers of this dark world and against the spiritual forces of evil in the heavenly realms. Therefore put on the full armor of God, so that when the day of evil comes, you may be able to stand your ground, and after you have done everything, to stand (Ephesians 6:12-13).

There is a plan of the enemy to destroy Christians, but there is also the plan of God. There are two plans at work here; one of the two plans will prevail in your life. Jesus told his disciples in the Gospel of Matthew 11:12, "The kingdom of heaven suffers violence, and the violent take it by force" (NKJV). In order to fulfill the full plan of God for your life, it will take violence and war in the spiritual realms. Christians who do not want to get wrinkles in their suits will not experience the glory of God coming to earth because it takes warriors. Christians who pray vain repetitive prayers will not see heaven come to earth. The enemy has his people praying strategically against the church, but I believe that God is raising up warriors who will crush the onslaught of the enemy with their worship and prayers. My prayer for you is that you will have a greater awareness of the warfare that surrounds us, and you will rise up as a warrior and help destroy the plan of the enemy.

OUR WEAPONS OF WARFARE

For though we walk in the flesh, we do not war after the flesh: (For the weapons of our warfare are not carnal, but mighty through God to the pulling down of strong holds;) Casting down imaginations, and every high thing that exalteth itself against the knowledge of God, and bringing into captivity every thought to the obedience of Christ (2 Corinthians 10:3-5, KJV).

I love the way the King James Version states this Scripture. We are not warring or wrestling against a human enemy. Our enemy is spiritual; therefore our weapons must be spiritual. We have the power of God vested in us to thwart every attack of the enemy. The enemy works mainly through what the KJV calls "strongholds." The root of this word in the Greek is *echo* which means "to have possession or control of." The word Paul uses here can be translated as "prison." It is our work to set people free from the enemy "having" their mind, and set them free from being kept in "prison."

An historical and military definition of the word "stronghold" gives us the picture of two countries at war. If two opposing countries went to war, one country would have a tough time invading the other country outright, but they could develop strongholds, sometimes called bridgeheads. They may send soldiers to covertly live among that country. These soldiers would live and work there. They would quietly and slowly bring supplies and other troops over to live covertly, also. This is a stronghold. Eventually they would have enough soldiers that had blended into that society to come out and fight. It would be similar to the Trojan horse used in the story of Achilles. They would have enemies that lived in their midst and now have overtaken them.

Satan can develop strongholds in our lives through sin and disobedience. Where there is quiet disobedience and compromise, there is also a stronghold with which the enemy can bring in his supplies covertly. There are many believers who are in "prison." Their minds have strongholds through which the enemy has connection points. The Apostle Paul tells us, "For the weapons of our warfare are not carnal but are mighty in God for pulling down strongholds" (2 Corinthians 10:4, NKJV).

CORPORATE REPENTANCE

The key to pulling down the spiritual strongholds in certain regions is closing the doorway to sin. This is accomplished through corporate repentance which was a common theme in the Old Testament. When sin was identified in the camp and the curse of God had come upon the camp, the people would corporately fast and pray. They would tear their clothes, put on sackcloth and ashes, and fast and pray. This is seen in Nehemiah when the Law was read to the people where there was weeping and repentance. The enemy has snares in the lives of Christians when there is unrepentant and unconfessed sin.

One of the keys to impacting our communities for Christ is knowing the history of that community. It is important to know what innocent bloodshed happened there. It is important to know if there was a strong Masonic influence in that community. It is important to know if racism and slavery saturated that city. You should also be current on what is happening in the community right now.

Spiritual warfare starts when the people of God come before Him repenting for the sins of that community and ask God to visit it. Churches need to fast for their community, crying and repenting before God for the past and present sins of the community. Our country has aborted millions of unborn babies and is destroying the fabric of a Biblical family. We have the largest pornography industries in the world and now child sex-trade is at an all-time high. There are more unchurched people in America than ever before. Warfare is real and the enemy is making a dent.

Where there is sin, there is the enemy. You may ask, "How do we know where the enemy is present?" Just look for sin. Cities are known for different sin. To the observer, one may see that Las Vegas is known primarily for gambling. L.A is known for extreme gang violence and prostitution. Washington D.C. has strong Masonic ties to the forefathers of this nation. You need to study the history of your city and region, and then bring your congregation together to fast and pray. It is the commitment of our church to pray every Wednesday for our community.

Some cities have hidden strongholds. I heard Pastor John Dawson share a story about this when he took a group of teens to share the gospel on the streets of South America. They saw no success all day. People would not listen and were opposed to the gospel. The team went back, fasted and prayed, and identified that there was a spirit of pride in that city. They humbled themselves with fasting and prayer and wept and cried for hours. The next day, they went out and many that they met wept and repented in the streets. As a result, revival broke out in the city![6] Once you can identify the unrepentant sin, you can speak against the enemy of that region. The strong man must be bound before one can have the spoils. There are curses over a city because the strong man still has power.

The Bible says, "No one can enter a strong man's house and plunder his goods, unless he first binds the strong man. And then he will plunder his house" (Mark 3:27, NKJV). Churches are seeking revival and people are seeking personal revival, but the strong man of their city and personal lives is still loose! There are different types of demonic forces that are tied to regions. I believe they are assigned to certain regions. Satan cannot be everywhere at once, so he is a master leader; he delegates all too well. We know that territorial demons exist because of Daniel 10:1-14:

> *In the third year of Cyrus king of Persia, a revelation was given to Daniel (who was called Belteshazzar). Its message was true and it concerned a great war. The understanding of the message came to him in a*

> *vision. At that time I, Daniel, mourned for three weeks. I ate no choice food; no meat or wine touched my lips; and I used no lotions at all until the three weeks were over. On the twenty-fourth day of the first month, as I was standing on the bank of the great river, the Tigris, I looked up and there before me was a man dressed in linen, with a belt of fine gold from Uphaz around his waist. His body was like topaz, his face like lightning, his eyes like flaming torches, his arms and legs like the gleam of burnished bronze, and his voice like the sound of a multitude. I, Daniel, was the only one who saw the vision; the men with me did not see it, but such terror overwhelmed them that they fled and hid themselves. So I was left alone, gazing at this great vision; I had no strength left, my face turned deathly pale and I was helpless. Then I heard him speaking, and as I listened to him, I fell into a deep sleep, my face to the ground. A hand touched me and set me trembling on my hands and knees. He said, "Daniel, you who are highly esteemed, consider carefully the words I am about to speak to you, and stand up, for I have now been sent to you." And when he said this to me, I stood up trembling. Then he continued, "Do not be afraid, Daniel. Since the first day that you set your mind to gain understanding and to humble yourself before your God, your words were heard, and I have come in response to them. But the prince of the Persian kingdom resisted me twenty-one days. Then Michael, one of the chief princes, came to help me, because I was detained there with the king of Persia. Now I have come to explain to you what will happen to your people in the future, for the vision concerns a time yet to come."*

This gives us a glimpse into the heavenly realm. Daniel was fasting and praying. He was seeking God for wisdom and understanding. The angel told Daniel that he could not bring the answer because the "prince of the Persian kingdom" resisted him. This was not a physical prince, but a spiritual one. The word *prince* here in the Hebrew means "one who leads hosts of others." This word can be translated to mean a government ruler, captain, or military head. This was a demon who was assigned to that region, and who possibly had rule or command over other demonic forces. We do know that he was responsible for keeping Daniel's blessing from coming forth.

The word *resist* can be translated from three Hebrew words put together which mean "appointed to oppose the presence of." This shows that this demonic force could possibly be appointed. At any rate, believers must be aware that there are forces at work outside of our five senses. Heaven was stopped from coming to earth because of this "prince." What blessings and prayers have been hindered in your life because of this? Pray and ask God for discernment on what regional or territorial forces are assigned against the breakout of your city. After you identify these strongmen, repent of the sin they have influence over. After this, continue in warfare.

A FRIENDLY WARNING

I want to stop for a commercial break. Many who experience spiritual warfare and want to impact their city for God end up looking for a demon behind every bush. Some people become more satan-conscious than God-conscious. They can identify demonic forces, but they never crack open the Word or seek the face of the Father. Satan is not the cause of everything and shouldn't be given too much credit. Be much more confident in God's plan than satan's plan. I am talking a lot about prayer and spiritual things, but we need to first pray, and then go to share the love of God with our communities.

Church leaders, don't tell your church you are going through warfare if you are not. If you are a pastor, do not elevate yourself and make statements like, "I am under a lot of warfare because I am the pastor." I once knew a church who blamed everything on spiritual warfare, and the only answer to any problem was prayer. Sometimes people make unwise decisions and the results are not the devil's fault. You can't pray your way out of consistently wrong decisions. Some things are the result of our own undoing. Man has responsibility, also. As you begin to dig deeper and come against the enemy, stop and ask yourself, "Am I balanced and walking in wisdom or am I chasing false demons and blaming my problems on the devil?"

THE HEAVENLY STRATEGY

> *Finally, be strong in the Lord and in his mighty power. Put on the full armor of God so that you can take your stand against the devil's schemes. For our struggle is not against flesh and blood, but against the rulers, against the authorities, against the powers of this dark world and against the spiritual forces of evil in the heavenly realms. Therefore put on the full armor of God, so that when the day of evil comes, you may be able to stand your ground, and after you have done everything, to stand. Stand firm then, with the belt of truth buckled around your waist, with the breastplate of righteousness in place, and with your feet fitted with the readiness that comes from the gospel of peace. In addition to all this, take up the shield of faith, with which you can extinguish all the flaming arrows of the evil one. Take the helmet of salvation and the sword of the Spirit, which is the word of God. And pray in the Spirit on all occasions with all kinds of prayers and requests. With this in mind, be alert and always keep on praying for all the Lord's people (Ephesians 6:10-18).*

Paul concludes his letter to the Ephesian church by encouraging them to stand and be strong in the Lord. He tells them to do this by putting on the armor of God. The Greek translation of this phrase can be rendered "the armor that is sourced in God Himself." Scholars refer to this as a genitive of source. This does not mean God has some armor lying around in heaven that He gives us. This does not mean that we have the armor. Many well-intentioned pastors preach that we must put on the armor of God every morning. They will tell you that you do this by quoting what the armor of God is. This teaching comes from a good heart, but the truth of this Scripture is saying, "Put on the armor that is sourced in God." This means that we only have access to the armor through our relationship with Christ. Christ is our armor. You cannot quote armor to get the armor on. Jesus Christ is our salvation, truth, peace, righteousness, and He gives us grace to share the gospel.

Paul used military terms to speak to the Ephesian culture since they were primarily military and retired military personnel, but he also used this to connote that believers must have a "militant" mind-set about their relationship with God. A majority of Christians are complacent about their relationship with Christ. They desire to know Him, but have made no action to move forward in knowing Him. Paul was sending a message to those believers that if they do not rise up and become warriors in the spiritual realm, they will be destroyed.

Verse 11 of Ephesians chapter six says, "Put on the full armor of God so that you may stand against the schemes of the devil." *Schemes* means a "carefully laid out plan." A believer must have great sensitivity in two areas; foremost, the working of God, and secondly, the working of the enemy. The enemy of our souls has devised a plan to destroy us. Paul told the church to put on the full, whole, and complete armor of God in order stand against the plans of the enemy.

He was writing some important and powerful Scriptures about spiritual warfare.

A believer must first have an unbroken, complete relationship with God before he or she can fight any battle. Paul gives four different ranks of demonic forces. There are not many other places in the New Testament where this is used, so I will be only as clear as the Bible is clear. Please understand that the Bible does not teach explicitly on this subject, but it does have enough for a believer to pay attention. Too many people have tried to teach things that this passage is not saying; I want to look at what it is saying. If you desire to bring heaven to earth in your personal life, here are some **PRACTICAL WAR TACTICS**:

1. We have a Supernatural Enemy.

> *For our struggle is not against flesh and blood, but against the rulers,* ***against the authorities, against the powers of this dark world and against the spiritual forces of evil in the heavenly realms****. Therefore put on the full armor of God, so that when the day of evil comes, you may be able to stand your ground, and after you have done everything, to stand (Ephesians 6:12-13).*

There is no way to fight a spiritual battle if we cannot overcome battles in the flesh. Christians are usually extremists when it comes to this issue of spiritual warfare. Either they dismiss the workings of demons and satan altogether, or they are spiritually crazy about these issues. We must have understanding. Paul prayed that the Colossians would have spiritual wisdom and understanding (Colossians 1:9). Our enemy is supernatural, so we must war in the supernatural realms. This type of Christian living is for an uncommon generation.

This type of war will cause you to go through spiritual boot camp. There is a point in a Christian's life when he or she must move from praying ordinary, flesh-driven prayers to the point where he or she begins to pray in the supernatural. The Bible tells us in Galatians, "Pray in the Spirit." Again, this is a topic of controversy. Denominations and groups have different meanings for this. Generally speaking, this means a prayer life that is reliant on the Spirit's prompting in prayer. A supernatural work needs supernatural Christians. Our enemy is not a man or man-made. Our enemy is a fallen angel whose minions operate in the heavenly realms. Know that our enemy is supernatural.

2. Be Militant about Your Relationship with God.

> *For our struggle is not against flesh and blood, but against the rulers, against the authorities, against the powers of this dark world and against the spiritual forces of evil in the heavenly realms.* ***Therefore put on the full armor of God****, so that when the day of evil comes, you may be able to stand your ground, and after you have done everything, to stand (Ephesians 6:12-13).*

Paul brings verses 12 and 13 together with "therefore." Since there is a supernatural enemy who operates in a supernatural realm we need to take specific action. Paul says, "Put on the full armor of God." It is interesting that the NIV translation says, "put on." When we hear this phrase we picture someone putting on a necklace or a hat. This phrase, *endyo*, in the Greek text, comes from "en" and "dyo." *En* is a preposition that has a common meaning of something being put in or on. *Dyo* is a word which traditionally means to clothe, or wear. It is also important to know that Paul uses the same terminology when he uses the phrases, "put on Christ," and "put on the new self." You cannot wake up in the morning and "put on Christ." It is an understanding and then living out that understanding. It is no different with this concept of the armor of God. You have to understand that you have it and then you need to live it out through a dynamic relationship with God.

At a glimpse, it seems that Paul is telling the Ephesians to throw on some armor from the closet. When we were saved did we "throw" on Christ? It was a conversion that started inside and worked its way outside. Paul is telling the Ephesians that they must cover themselves from the inside out with a relationship with God. You cannot get up each morning and quote the armor and think that you are covered. This is an inner working of the Holy Spirit that comes from relationship. I stated earlier that the source of the armor is God Himself. You cannot go anywhere else to get it. Since there is a great host of enemies on the other side, we must become passionate and militant about our relationship with the Father. All the provision we need against any battle is in Him. The provision is not in the memorizing of armor, but in the power that comes from a relationship with Him. If that relationship is severed, we may as well give up. There is a host of enemies in the supernatural, therefore we must move into the supernatural through a deepening of our relationship with the Father. Through that relationship we are clothed with spiritual armor.

3. The Anti-Assignment.

> *For our struggle is not against flesh and blood, but against the rulers, against the authorities, against the powers of this dark world and against the spiritual forces of evil in the heavenly realms. Therefore put on the full armor of God,* ***<u>so that</u>*** *when the day of evil comes, you may be able to stand your ground, and after you have done everything, to stand (Ephesians 6:12-13).*

You don't have to go looking for the enemy. The enemy has ranks of demons who are assigned to destroy your life. Again, there are two plans in the universe; the plan of God and the plan of satan. God has a plan for all of us; satan's plan is to make sure that God's plan is not fulfilled. Satan has desires for this world, also. Remember the battle is about who is going to be in charge. Satan wanted to be in charge, so God sent Him to earth where he roamed and ruled earth with his demons. God then created time and put man on the earth. Desiring worship himself, satan despised God's creation. So, the cosmic battle is for who will receive worship. Either you worship God or the devil; there is no middle ground.

The enemy's plan is to pull you out of relationship with God. Paul tells the Ephesian church to get militant about their relationship with God and become supernatural Christians. He inserts the phrase, "so that..." which tells them there is a purpose. He finishes the phrase by telling them why: so they can be ready when the day of evil comes. There is a lot of debate about the phrase, "the day of evil." Is this a particular day? Is Paul referring to the possible tribulation period? Is this a figure of speech? I want to look at this verse as a figure of speech. Paul says that a day is coming when evil will pursue you personally. There are tests and trials where God will seek to promote you and the enemy will seek to pervert you. We do not need to be spiritual demon hunters, but we need to be sensitive and aware that the enemy is working. There may be battles that arise where the enemy is directly involved. When we are able to recognize this, we can go to the source of the issue. Satan's goal is to stop God's will from being done on earth **just as it is in heaven**.

Satan knows what is going on in heaven; he has been there. He knows that we are God's prized possession, and that God has chosen us to be the invaders of earth with His love. Satan hates heaven and the worship of Almighty God. He has devised a plan to destroy the funnel from heaven to earth. We are heaven's funnel; God funnels heaven to earth through us. If Satan can destroy us, then he can prevent heaven from reaching earth. May God open our eyes up to the supernatural realm and the strategy of the enemy.

4. Be Unmoved and Unstoppable in Your Walk with God.

> *For our struggle is not against flesh and blood, but against the rulers, against the authorities, against the powers of this dark world and against the spiritual forces of evil in the heavenly realms. Therefore put on the full armor of God, so that when the day of evil comes,* ***you may be able to stand your ground, and after you have done everything, to stand*** *(Ephesians 6:12-13).*

Satan can only have what we give him. He cannot take ground, but we can give it to him by giving ourselves over to sin. Paul tells the Ephesian church to stand their ground. During the time Paul wrote this letter, when opposing armies fought they were protecting ground and legal boundaries for their country. Joshua's battles in the Old Testament were for territory or ground. Our battle is the same today. God has given us an inheritance. He has poured everything we need into our lives, but it is up to us to protect and keep what He has given us. Paul told Timothy, 'Guard the deposit that is inside of you.'

There are a ton of believers who are standing their ground, but the enemy does not have to stop them because they are not going anywhere! It is time that we not only stand our ground, but take what the enemy has taken from us. An unstoppable army is able to plunder the spoils of the enemy. We have given the enemy our time, energy, money, families, and anointing. It is time that we tell him that he must restore what has been taken. Again, Jesus said in Matthew 11:12, "The kingdom of God suffers violence, but the violent take it by force" (NKJV). Jesus was saying that it is the ones who are violent about their walk with God and violent with the enemy that will be able to see the power of God come forth. In this war we are in, we must stand our ground. Be a warrior. You will never outgrow spiritual warfare; you must simply learn to fight.

CONCLUDING THOUGHTS

Revelation chapter 12 reveals to us that there is a war going on in heaven. There is constant war in the supernatural realm. There are assignments of the enemy created by satan to destroy God's plan for our lives. Some denominations say, "It doesn't matter." Others say, "We must have warfare banners and march around the sanctuary." I think the key is to be aware and live out the fullness of our relationship with the Lord.

But there is a generation that is entering into genuine warfare with the enemy. There is a close connection between worship and warfare. The worshippers of the Old Testament were on the frontline. They were sent out to the battle. It is time that our churches, families, and individual Christians stand and take the ground that has been lost for centuries. This will not look pretty.

My prayer for you is this: "Lord, open their eyes to see the supernatural realm. Help this believer to know that there are forces at work that we cannot see. Remove the lies. Remove the lie that says this doesn't matter. Also Lord, remove the lie that everything is spiritual warfare. Give them a proper perspective. I pray that they will go and break the territorial spirits of their region. I pray that they will walk in your power in all that they do, in the name of Jesus. Amen."

End Notes:
[5] Author Unknown. "Common Ground, Vol. 10 No. 7." SermonIllustrations.com.
[6] Dawson, John. *Taking Our Cities for God.* Pg. 34. Lake Mary, FL: Charisma House. 1989.

REFLECTION GUIDE

Take some time to reflect on these questions:

What is one element you read from this chapter that challenged you? Why?

What do you need to change in your thinking to apply the principles from this chapter?

What did you have the most trouble receiving because of previous teachings? Why?

What did you like the most about this chapter? Why?

CHAPTER 5

INFUSED WITH PURITY

After this I looked, and there before me was a door standing open in heaven. And the voice I had first heard speaking to me like a trumpet said, "Come up here, and I will show you what must take place after this." At once I was in the Spirit, and there before me was a throne in heaven with someone sitting on it. And the one who sat there had the appearance of jasper and ruby. A rainbow that shown like an emerald, encircled the throne. Surrounding the throne were twenty-four other thrones, and seated on them were twenty-four elders. They were dressed in white and had crowns of gold on their heads. From the throne came flashes of lightning, rumblings and peals of thunder. In front of the throne, seven lamps were blazing. These are the seven spirits of God. Also in front of the throne there was what looked like a sea of glass, clear as crystal. In the center, around the throne, were four living creatures, and they were covered with eyes, in front and in back. The first living creature was like a lion, the second was like an ox, the third had a face like a man, the fourth was like a flying eagle. Each of the four living creatures had six wings and was covered with eyes all around, even under its wings. Day and night they never stop saying:
"Holy, holy, holy is the Lord God Almighty,
who was, and is, and is to come." (Revelation 4:1-8).

MY CALL TO PURITY

When I was first saved, I was asked to play in a "Christian" band. These guys looked like Christians, sang Christian songs, and went to church so I decided to join the band and go on a mini-tour with them. I had been cleansed and delivered from a life of drugs, alcohol, and gross sin, and I was fired up for Jesus. When the replacement drummer told me that I had a "youth group fire" and that it would soon die I knew something was wrong. On that tour, they pulled out cigarettes. This shocked me because I had just been delivered from this. Our biggest altercation was when they were watching MTV® in the hotel room. They laughed about how "hot" this singer was and how many times they gave themselves sexual pleasure while watching her video. I finally stood up and told them what the Bible said, and they laughed and mocked me. Their parents were pastors and deacons, and they told me that they did not want to hear any of that stuff. I began to smoke on that tour, and my morals slipped.

I returned that Sunday to my home church. There was a traveling evangelist named Kathy Sandlin that had come to speak. She made this one statement: "Purity equals power. If you want to see God's power, He needs to see your purity." After this service, I went home and spent some time in prayer. God told me, "Kevin, if you will quit that band and pursue purity, I will use you greatly in another band, a band you will start." I made that decision to obey the Lord and started a band of my own. Three years later my new band was touring and had recorded three albums. I had the opportunity to be interviewed on TBN and the Inspirational channel. God showed great favor, and His power was demonstrated through my desire for purity.

TRUE HOLINESS

The Holiness Movement started in the 1800's and still pervades the southeast part of the United States where there are many denominations represented. The leaders of the "old school" holiness movement prided themselves on outward holiness, but often ignored the true holiness that pleases God. They often hated people of other races, and the husbands would treat their wives like slaves. Sins of the flesh were condemned, but the sins of the spirit, such as jealousy, envy, strife and dissension, were overlooked.

Holiness and purity are a requirement for the call of God. Many people see holiness as an outward conformation to rules, but being holy is being wholly given over to God. If you obey seventy-five rules of dress-code, but hate a person of the opposite race, then you are unholy. We live in a generation that is different. I wish that teaching holiness was as easy as teaching women not to cut their hair. Women face many more obstacles today. Many do not have fathers to teach and help them. They are exposed to false standards of models on TV. Many struggle with issues that were not even around in the 1950's. God's call to purity is not what you don't do, but it is wrapped up in what you pursue.

GOD'S REQUIREMENT FOR THE CALL IS PURITY

Minister Robert Murray M'Cheyne wrote to Dan Edwards after the latter's ordination as a missionary, "In great measure, according to the purity and perfections of the instrument, will be the success. It is not great talents God blesses, but a great likeness to Jesus. A holy minister is an awful weapon in the hand of God."[7] God cannot mightily use an unclean vessel. This statement does not mean that God uses only perfect people, but this means that God uses people who are submitted to Him.

Holiness is not the absence of imperfection but the result of daily surrender. People who qualify for the call are those who will deal with anything that causes them to be impure. If you have fifty gallons of pure water and drop one ounce of arsenic into the water, then all fifty gallons are impure. In a message entitled, "From this Day Forward," Pastor Craig Groeschel of *www.LifeChurch.tv* said that impurity is, "not that your corn touched your mashed potatoes. That will happen. Impurity is a cat using the bathroom in your mashed potatoes. It is not dust getting in your bottle of water, but rather poison getting in your water."

In his book entitled ***Habitudes 1***, Dr. Tim Elmore shared the "Laptop Principle." A laptop merely puts out what we put in. It is what he calls the "G.I.G.O" principle. That means, "Garbage In/Garbage Out."[8] What people put into their lives is what they will get out. There are numerous people who attempt to live a life mixed with the darkness of the world and the light of Christ. They have learned the Christian talk and the Christian walk, but have not learned personal purity.

This type of mind-set comes from becoming desensitized to sin over a considerable amount of time. Things that we once considered impure over time begin to look "alright." The biggest enemy of purity is the mind-set that makes us think we are able to judge what is pure and right in our own eyes. If we justify that the Bible does not speak of it therefore we can partake in it, we are on the wrong path.

We are under attack in this generation. We need ministers who are armed with "wholiness." We need people who give God their whole hearts and lives, and not just their gifts. For earth to be infused with heaven, we will need a revival of purity among all people. We kill the prophets and stone the apostles of God; we do not want to hear that we have sin. In our present day, we have a movement of TV preachers who want you to believe you are the greatest thing ever. They want you to believe that you can do no wrong. Don't get me wrong, their intention is good. We need to know our standing with God. We need to know that we are His righteousness. We need to know we have potential, but we must also personally confront our sins. If you read the Bible, you will see that this is a real concept. And you know what? You won't like hearing it. Your flesh will fight it. You will find "cut and paste" Scriptures to dispute what I am telling you. If a minister touches on these things, we are ready to give seven reasons why we can do what we want to do. This generation is a generation who is like the one in Judges where "everyone did what was right in their own eyes." We must begin to sing the heavenly song, "Holy, Holy, Holy."

Read what Paul Borthwick, minister and author, has to say:

> We can supplement our accountability to others by reading slowly through literature designed to challenge our Christian maturity. Consider, as an example, these questions related to sexual purity that I had to read carefully as I read Kent Hughes' ***Liberating Ministry from the Success Syndrome***:
>
> 1. Are we being desensitized by the present evil world? Do things that once shocked us now pass us by with little notice? Have our sexual ethics slackened?
> 2. Where do our minds wander when we have no duties to perform?
> 3. What are we reading? Are there books or magazines or files in our libraries that we want no one else to see?
> 4. What are we renting at the local video stores (or Netflix®)? How many hours do we spend watching TV? How much adultery did we

watch last week? How many murders? How many did we watch with our children?

5. How many chapters of the Bible did we read last week?[9]

In order to walk in a greater level of purity we must place ourselves under a greater level of accountability. It takes us allowing people in our lives to ask us the tough questions about purity. These questions are great for an accountability small group.

My friend Jim was teaching children's church one Sunday when the topic was "Garbage In/Garbage Out." He began to ask the children about their lives. Ninety percent of the children, from age six to eleven, said that they had watched horror movies and movies that had extensive killing. These children could quote these movies. They also shared that they had thoughts of killing others because of this. As their parents were worshiping in the sanctuary, they were sharing the truth of their real spirituality at home. We must repent of our sins that we have passed on to our children. As you are reading this book, do an inventory of your life. What is the one ounce of "arsenic" in your Christian life that is causing you to be impure? Where is the cat taking a dump in your mashed potatoes?

PURITY DEVELOPS CHARACTER

During a class with Dr. Bobby Clinton, he shared with us that very few leaders finish well. He said that was mainly because the leaders lacked character. They allowed little things into their life that hurt them. We cannot develop character without developing purity. Character is who you are in the dark when no one is looking. God chooses people and uses people based primarily on their character. If God is going to use this generation, then we must be one that pursues purity and character.

This point is greatly illustrated when two seminary students discussing purity walked by a sign in a store one day that said, "SUIT—SLIGHTLY SOILED and GREATLY REDUCED IN VALUE." When we let the sin reign in our lives, it greatly reduces the way in which God can use us.[10] Prophetic songwriter of our day, Jason Upton, says, "We cannot have true victory without hearts of purity."

To stress the importance of the word *purity*, we must know what it truly means. *Purity* literally means "things that are sacred unto God for His use." The word "holiness" also comes from the same root word as "purity" which is *hagios*. God is calling us to be ready for His use. This also means everything that we come in contact with must be set apart to Him. I want to show you a leader in the Bible who exemplified this principle.

ISAIAH'S PURIFYING EXPERIENCE

The prophet Isaiah records his calling in Isaiah chapter six. This is a great picture of God's purifying work in His leaders. When God calls a generation He always starts with the leaders. The first thing God does in these leaders is to purify them. Let's take a look at this passage:

> *In the year that King Uzziah died, I saw the Lord seated on a throne, high and exalted, and the train of his robe filled the temple. Above him were seraphs, each with six wings: With two wings they covered their faces, with two they covered their feet, and with two they were flying. And they were calling to one another: "Holy, holy, holy is the LORD Almighty; the whole earth is full of his glory." At the sound of their voices the doorposts and thresholds shook and the temple was filled with smoke. "Woe to me!" I cried. "I am ruined! For I am a man of unclean lips, and I live among a people of unclean lips,*

> *and my eyes have seen the King, the LORD Almighty." Then one of the seraphim flew to me with a live coal in his hand, which he had taken with tongs from the altar. With it he touched my mouth and said, "See, this has touched your lips; your guilt is taken away and your sin atoned for." Then I heard the voice of the Lord saying, "Whom shall I send? And who will go for us?"*
>
> *And I said, "Here am I. Send me!" He said, "Go and tell this people:*
>
> *"'Be ever hearing, but never understanding; be ever seeing, but never perceiving.' Make the heart of this people calloused; make their ears dull and close their eyes. Otherwise they might see with their eyes, hear with their ears, understand with their hearts, and turn and be healed" (Isaiah 6:1-10, NIV).*

Isaiah goes through the first five chapters of his book talking about prophecy and what God wants to do, and then suddenly he stops and shares the event surrounding his personal calling. He pauses the movie and puts on the prequel. This chapter is the prequel to his calling.

This is a powerful passage with so many parallels and messages in it, but I want to look at the importance of purity in this passage. Notice that the angels were singing "Holy, Holy, Holy" to one another. This is the sound of heaven. When Isaiah hears the sound of heaven, and especially the sound of purity, he notices what type of person he is. We are wondering why people are not repenting and coming under the conviction of the Holy Spirit. Often, this is mainly because we are not in awe of the holiness and purity of God. I love what my wife said about singing unto God, "It is easy to worship with all your heart when you are singing to God about His attributes. It seems harder to worship when you are singing a song about dancing, getting blessings, or something God just wants to do. When you are singing about the goodness of God something begins to happen in the atmosphere." Isaiah was in the presence and power of God. It was during this experience in which God called him. Isaiah came to the realization that he was a man of unclean lips, so the angel took a coal and put it on his lips.

This amazed me when I first read it because he is a prophet! I don't think he went around swearing and talking smack to folks. He was a man separated unto God, but did not know what was going on in heaven. He knew what God said, but did not know what God was saying to him personally. What happened to Isaiah was that he was purified and, he could then hear the call. It is very interesting to note that when God called him, He was not specifically calling him; He was just asking, possibly the Trinity, "Who will go for Us, whom shall I send?" Isaiah overheard this in the throne room and answered the call. There is a series of **events that led to Isaiah answering the call**:

1. The Revelation of God in His Life.

"In the year that King Uzziah died, I saw the Lord, high and exalted, seated on a throne; and the train of his robe filled the temple." (Isaiah 6:1).

Isaiah "saw" God high and lifted up. In order for us to move to what God has for us, we must open our eyes to who He is. Everything that is needed from God is sourced inside of Him. There are Christian men praying for purity from pornography not realizing that freedom from this is sourced in their revelation of who God is. If God is only a Savior, then that is all you will settle for, but if God is your Deliverer and Victorious Warrior, then you will be able get that from Him, too.

In Matthew 16 Jesus asks the disciples, "Who do you say that I am?" Peter answered and told him, "You are the Christ, the Son of the Living God" (NKJV). Jesus then told him that he received this by revelation and then Jesus called him "Peter" or "rock." He said that Peter would no longer be called "Simon" or "reed" (shaken in the wind), but a rock. Peter was able to have this new revelation because he had a deeper revelation of who Christ was in his life. The secret is not what we think about Jesus, but who He is in our lives. Paul prayed in Ephesians that "the eyes of our understanding be enlightened." The first step in answering the call is being a people with an ever increasing illumination of the true nature of God.

2. The Revelation of Sin that Was Holding Him Back.

> *And they were calling to one another: "Holy, holy, holy is the LORD Almighty; the whole earth is full of his glory." At the sound of their voices the doorposts and thresholds shook and the temple was filled with smoke. "Woe to me!" I cried. "I am ruined! For I am a man of unclean lips, and I live among a people of unclean lips, and my eyes have seen the King, the LORD Almighty." Then one of the seraphim flew to me with a live coal in his hand, which he had taken with tongs from the altar. With it he touched my mouth and said, "See, this has touched your lips; your guilt is taken away and your sin atoned for" (Isaiah 6:3-7).*

Isaiah must have had some sort of issue with "unclean lips." We will never know what this was, but we do know that God brought it to the surface and made Isaiah deal with what would hold him back from declaring God's Word. Isaiah would never have heard the call if he had not dealt with his unclean lips. Isaiah confessed and repented of his sin before

God and the angel cleansed him. If we are going to answer the call of God for our generation and see God's power inhabit earth, we must begin to repent and confess our sin before God.

People are comfortable with sin until they enter the true presence of God. God intends to develop us to our full potential so God will reveal to us anything that hinders our full potential. God will not allow even one of the smallest things to get in the way of His relationship with you. If we decide to hide our sin, blame the culture and past circumstances, then God will bypass us and find someone else He can use. When God is revealed to us and our hindrances are revealed we must begin to deal with them so we can hear the call.

3. The Revelation of the Call.

> *Then I heard the voice of the Lord saying, "Whom shall I send? And who will go for us?" And I said, "Here am I. Send me!" He said, "Go and tell this people: "'Be ever hearing, but never understanding; be ever seeing, but never perceiving.' Make the heart of this people calloused; make their ears dull and close their eyes. Otherwise they might see with their eyes, hear with their ears, understand with their hearts, and turn and be healed" (Isaiah 6:8-10).*

Isaiah was able to clearly hear the call of God and gain a burden for His people. Notice that God's call was not to Isaiah, but His call was to the heavens. He called out in heaven first, "Who shall go for us? Whom shall I send?" The move of God in Isaiah's generation did not originate on earth. Everything God does on earth starts with a word in heaven. The Bible says in the Gospel of John chapter 1 verse 1, "In the beginning was the Word. The Word was with God and the Word was God" (NKJV). God sent His Word, Jesus, to change the situation on earth. Isaiah heard the sound of heaven and responded.

In order for this generation to fulfill the call of God, we must be people who are in touch with what God is saying from heaven. Isaiah is one of the most prophetic books when dealing with the future coming of Christ. Scholars say Isaiah is the most Messianic prophet. Isaiah was able to prophesy about the Word coming to change earth because he had a word from heaven to change it. We need a prophetic generation to come forth who can announce the call of heaven. What is God's desire for your city? Your country? What is God saying about your region right now? How does God feel about your workplace? Heaven is sounding forth right now. Will you take time to hear what the Lord is speaking specifically to you, or will you allow worldly pleasures to push you further away from the heart of God?

THE PROCESS OF PURITY

At some point and time, every leader must ask himself or herself, "Is it really worth it to go through with this?" There is a price to pay for walking in purity and there is a price to pay for not walking in purity. I can say that the rewards for walking in purity are much greater. There have been great Christian leaders who recently fell from grace. Whether it was adultery, wronged divorce, or financial greed, they all had the Holy Spirit ask them, "Is it really worth it?" As you face temptation and sin on a daily basis, ask yourself that same question.

A poll that was performed by **Focus on the Family** stated that 18 percent of Christian men polled had admitted to using internet pornography that week. A Gallop poll conducted stated that 30% of ministers in America regularly viewed pornography, and another poll that was conducted by Promise Keepers® said that one in three men had fallen into pornography the week after attending the Promise Keepers® event.[11] Make no mistake my friend, purity is a process. You will not be completely whole at an altar call. It will take accountability with trusted colleagues. It will take reading books on the issues that seek to displace your purity. It will take perseverance. As you read earlier, there is an attack on this generation, therefore we must be guarded. How much is your purity before God worth?

End Notes:

[7] Paul Borthwick. *Leading the Way*. Navpress: 1989, pp. 65.

[8] Elmore, Tim. *Habitudes 1: Art of Self-Leadership*. Poet Gardner Publishers. 2010.

[9] Paul Borthwick, *Leading the Way*, Navpress, 1989, pp. 120-121.

[10] Unknown. "Purity." SermonIllustrations.com.

[11] Focus on the Family. "Pornography and Clergy." 2005. WCLN 107.3. Radio.

REFLECTION GUIDE

Take some time to reflect on these questions:

What is one element you read from this chapter that challenged you? Why?

What do you need to change in your thinking to apply the principles from this chapter?

What did you have the most trouble receiving because of previous teachings? Why?

What did you like the most about this chapter? Why?

CHAPTER 6

INFUSED WITH VICTORY

After this I heard what sounded like the roar of a great multitude in heaven shouting:

> *"Hallelujah! Salvation and glory and power belong to our God, for true and just are his judgments. He has condemned the great prostitute who corrupted the earth by her adulteries. He has avenged on her the blood of his servants."*

And again they shouted:

> *"Hallelujah! The smoke from her goes up for ever and ever."*

The twenty-four elders and the four living creatures fell down and worshiped God, who was seated on the throne. And they cried:

> *"Amen, Hallelujah!"*

Then a voice came from the throne, saying:

> *"Praise our God, all you his servants, you who fear him, both small and great!"*

Then I heard what sounded like a great multitude, like the roar of rushing waters and like loud peals of thunder, shouting:

> *"Hallelujah! For our Lord God Almighty reigns. Let us rejoice and be glad and give him glory! For the wedding of the Lamb has come, and his bride has made herself ready. Fine linen, bright and clean, was given her to wear."*

(Fine linen stands for the righteous acts of the saints.)

Then the angel said to me, "Write: 'Blessed are those who are invited to the wedding supper of the Lamb!'"And he added, "These are the true words of God."

At this I fell at his feet to worship him. But he said to me, "Do not do it! I am a fellow servant with you and with your brothers who hold to the testimony of Jesus. Worship God! For the testimony of Jesus is the spirit of prophecy."

I saw heaven standing open and there before me was a white horse, whose rider is called Faithful and True. With justice he judges and makes war. His eyes are like blazing fire, and on his head are many crowns. He has a name written on him that no one knows but he himself. He is dressed in a robe dipped in blood, and his name is the Word of God. The armies of heaven were following him, riding on white horses and dressed in fine linen, white and clean. Out of his mouth comes a sharp sword with which to strike down the nations. "He will rule them with an iron scepter." He treads the winepress of the fury of the wrath of God Almighty. On his robe and on his thigh he has this name written: KING OF KINGS AND LORD OF LORDS.

And I saw an angel standing in the sun, who cried in a loud voice to all the birds flying in midair, "Come, gather together for the great supper of God, so that you may eat the flesh of kings, generals, and mighty men, of horses and their riders, and the flesh of all people, free and slave, small and great." Then I saw the beast and the kings of the earth and their armies gathered together to make war against the rider on the horse and his army. But the beast was captured, and with him the false prophet who had performed the miraculous signs on his behalf. With these signs he had deluded those who had received the mark of the beast and worshiped his image. The two of them were thrown alive into the fiery lake of burning sulfur. The rest of them were killed with the sword that came out of the mouth of the rider on the horse, and all the birds gorged themselves on their flesh (Revelation 19:1-21).

THE MESSAGE OF THE GOSPEL

This mother had been waiting for months. Each day as she would dump her pots of cooking and washing water outside, she would look intently to the west in hopes that the army had won. The eerie silence of each closing day would carry her imagination to extremes. Her only child was fighting in this battle. There was a lot in this battle for her. If the foreign army won the battle, her country would become captive to theirs and be slaves; she may end up burying her child. She waited patiently for the news of victory. She waited to see her son once more, and she waited to hear of the future of her country. Would she be a slave?

The setting is 2000 years ago in the Middle East when there were no sophisticated communication systems. No one could simply pick up a phone and call. There was no wireless café with CNN®'s broadcast of the war. She only heard rumors in the village where she lived. Letters were not allowed to be sent by the soldiers at this time. Since this was such a big battle, they forbade anyone coming back to the camp until all was said and done.

Months passed and still each day this woman would wait and watch. She was waiting for the runner. This runner would bring news back from the battle. He would enter the village shouting victory or defeat. Finally, one evening as she continued her same routine, a young man came close to the village running and shouting. Dust was like a cloud all around him. Excitement rose up within the heart of this mother. The villagers all came out of their homes to hear the news. The runner was shouting, "Euangellion! Euangellion! Euangellion! (*u-ahn-gel-lee-ahn*)" Shouts rose up from across the village. The mother did not know the status of her son, but she did know this: the victory had been secured. They would not be slaves. They had dominion over their enemy.

The Greek word for *gospel* in the New Testament is "euangellion."[12] This word generally means "good news." If we are able to look a bit deeper at the meaning in its historical context, we find that this word meant, "We have the victory!" The story you just read was a fictitious story that paints a picture of the historical meaning of the word "gospel." This word existed before Jesus used it. It historically meant to the people of that time that victory had been established.

Jesus did not come to earth to just tell us about some "good news." Good news is that your friend received a raise or someone got a great deal on a new car. Jesus used this word to allow us to understand that He has already defeated all the works of darkness. We are not fighting for victory; we are fighting from a place of victory. My friends, Jesus came to earth to declare that we are already victorious in Him. Many Christians believe that they have to get the victory over the devil. They do not understand that they first have positional victory, and they then can have experiential victory. We have it already!

The gospel is a gospel of victory. The next time you hear that it means good news, take time to let it sink in what this good news meant to the lady in the story. She did not have to be a slave to the enemy! She was free. If anything, now, the other country had to be slaves to her country.

OCCUPY AND INFUSE

He said therefore, A certain nobleman went into a far country to receive for himself a kingdom, and to return. And he called his ten servants, and delivered them ten pounds, and said unto them, Occupy till I come (Luke 19:12-13, KJV).

When a majority of believers read these Scriptures they think of using their talents for God. Other generic thoughts are that *occupy* means to sit back and wait until Jesus returns. Luke records this as Jesus' last parable before His triumphal entry into Jerusalem where He was making a statement to His disciples: "Take ground and move forward." The word *occupy* literally means, "do business, or gain."[13] This can be applied to all of life. God has given us victory and has called us as a people to occupy. He has called us to be a people who take ground, not those who lose ground. Again, we are fighting from victory, not for victory. Jesus did pay it all. He also defeated and disarmed every principality and power that is in heaven or on earth. The disciples took him literally. How do we know this? Read the book of Acts and see what you think.

AN EXAMPLE FROM LIFE

For several years, the USA fought a war in Iraq. They captured the tyrannical dictator and overthrew his government. After the war was won and the victory secured, we are helping the Iraqi people establish democracy. We do not have to fight for victory anymore; we are simply fighting from a place of victory. Now we are enforcing the victory.

The Christian church must lose the victim mind-set. We sing pitiful hymns that talk about escaping to heaven. I heard one hymn that told Jesus we were waving a white flag for Him to come back and get us. That signifies defeat. "The world is just too bad," they say. This sounds spiritual, but it is far from biblical. Jesus is King now and forever. It is true that the Kingdom of God has not been fully established on earth yet, but we are to pray and usher in the Kingdom. Believers must understand that the gospel of Jesus Christ is not for a defeated army. The gospel means that Jesus stepped onto planet Earth declaring that we have all the victory we will ever need in Him.

WHAT THIS DOES NOT MEAN...

Now what I'm saying does not mean that we will never have trials or tribulation. I am also not saying that we will never suffer. I'm not saying that we will not struggle financially for some seasons. What I am saying is that we must know that we do not have to "pray through" for victory because we already have it. If believers would receive this revelation and start enforcing their victory, we would see a shift. We have positional victory. In Iraq, we possessed positional victory. That didn't mean that we did not still have to fight. Some denominations believe that once you get saved you can just glide into heaven. As believers, we must daily let the devil know that we are victorious. As we begin to *enforce* the victory Jesus won for us, we will *experience* victory.

FROM THE WORD

Joshua and the children of Israel are a great example of this principle. God promised them that the land of Canaan was their land. He told them victory was theirs if they would step out and fight. The children of Israel wandered forty years with this promise. At one point, they sent spies into the land. Two of the spies were Joshua and Caleb. Listen to the two confessions:

Then they told him, and said: "We went to the land where you sent us. It truly flows with milk and honey, and this is its fruit. Nevertheless the people who dwell in the land are strong; the cities are fortified and very large; moreover we saw the descendants of Anak there. The Amalekites dwell in the land of the South; the Hittites, the Jebusites, and the Amorites dwell in the mountains; and the Canaanites dwell by the sea and along the banks of the Jordan."

Then Caleb quieted the people before Moses, and said, "Let us go up at once and take possession, for we are well able to overcome it."

But the men who had gone up with him said, "We are not able to go up against the people, for they are stronger than we." And they gave the children of Israel a bad report of the land which they had spied out, saying, "The land through which we have gone as spies is a land that devours its inhabitants, and all the people whom we saw in it are men of great stature. There we saw the giants (the descendants of Anak came from the giants); and we were like grasshoppers in our own sight, and so we were in their sight" (Numbers 13:27-33, KJV).

A few verses later, Joshua exhorts the people to move forward and take possession of the land. They did not like it and wanted to stone him. Do you see the mind-set here? Eight of the ten spies did not believe that God had already given them the victory. They didn't believe they had positional victory, and they had never tasted victory experientially. Circumstances, obstacles, and outward forces shaped their thinking. This is no different from the church today. Christians are still singing songs about escaping "giants." Some have given in to the fable that they are not made to live victorious. They would rather settle for the life they have or revert back to their old life. The children of Israel began to shout that they wanted to go back to Egypt. Their lack of understanding of this concept of victory hindered them from walking into the Promised Land.

THE STEPS TO ACTUALIZING THIS VICTORY

As I said before, you are victorious in your position in Christ. When you were saved, you were made victorious because Christ has the victory. You may be addicted to something right now, you may be suffering depression, or all hell may be breaking loose in your life, but no matter what you are going through, you are victorious!

This is a great story that will help you understand the idea I am trying to portray. A farmer found a baby eagle in the forest. He carried the baby eagle back to his farm with the chickens. For years the eagle lived with the chickens, and he learned to act like them. As the eagle grew, the farmer wanted to try and release him back into the wild. He picked the eagle up and threw him in the air only to see him fall to the ground and return with the chickens. He finally took the eagle to a high mount and allowed the eagle to see other eagles. When the eagle saw other eagles soaring, he knew at that point what he was meant to do, so he took off and soared with the other eagles.

We are a lot like that eagle. Even though we are children of God and victorious in all things, we still act like chickens!

Victory is a process. I want to spell out the word victory and give you a breakdown of the process of victory.

EXPERIENCING V-I-C-T-O-R-Y

V—Victory is Actualized through Community

> *From whom the whole body, joined and knit together by what every joint supplies, according to the effective working by which every part does its share, causes growth of the body for the edifying of itself in love (Ephesians 4:16, NKJV).*

If I had one point to give you about victory it would be this: developing relationships with strong believers who believe in you is the greatest investment you can make. My life was changed in my early twenties by a group of guys I worked with in youth ministry. We challenged each other. We would call each other up and pray for each other. The youth pastor would invite me to seek God with him, and I would take off work to fast and pray with him. We held each other accountable.

Ephesians says that we are the body of Christ. Paul goes on to say in Ephesians 4 that we are "knit together by what every joint supplies." Christians who walk in victory have people who supply them and people they supply. They are literally conduits for the grace of God to flow through. I thank God for the men and women of God who supply me. I have had many of the ones I supply thank me. In order to walk out the plan and purpose of God and see actual victory one must search for "suppliers."

You will find yourself in the most trouble when you separate yourself from other believers. As a matter of fact, the first sign that I look for in a believer who is trying to walk away from Christ is they stop coming to church. Church by itself cannot save anyone, but there are many "suppliers" at church. I see people who are backsliding isolate themselves from leaders and friends. They offer great excuses saying the church is full of hypocrites. They are ready to write the next book, ***101 Reasons Why We Don't Have to Go to a Church***. Do you have to go to church to be a Christian? No, you don't have to go to be saved, but there are other reasons that you need to go. Your choice to attend a worship gathering with other believers is to supply and be supplied by others. Proverbs 18:1(a) states, "A man that isolates himself seeks only his own desire" (NKJV). Do not isolate yourself. Intentionally put yourself among people who can help you go to a level that you could not go to by yourself.

I—Intentional Spirituality

> *But this I say: He who sows sparingly will also reap sparingly, and he who sows bountifully will also reap bountifully. So let each one give as he purposes in his heart, not grudgingly or of necessity; for God loves a cheerful giver. And God is able to make all grace abound toward you, that you, always having all sufficiency in all things, may have an abundance for every good work (2 Corinthians 9:6-8, NKJV).*

There are two types of spirituality in the body of Christ: intentional and unintentional. Many believers are unintentional about their walk with God. Their time, money and relationships are not under the lordship of Christ. They may read the Bible or pray, but it is when they find the time and when they are comfortable doing it. I call these unintentional Christians. They see growth and know the Word, but you never see great measures of destiny fulfilled in their lives. There is never lasting fruit or impact.

Intentional Christians separate their time. They make time with God. The time with God that they have is of great quality. Spend enough time in the secret place with God to create a memory of it. Every bit of time with God should be special. I recently talked with a guy who proclaimed that he had no time to journal and write down what God was saying to him from Scripture. He said work and life were too demanding. I spent a couple of days with him and realized that he had time for surfing the net, playing music, and lollygagging. In order to have experiential victory one must be very intentional about their walk with God.

My suggestion for you is to set goals. Write down what yearly, quarterly, monthly, and weekly goals you would like to accomplish. Have those that are your "suppliers" look over those goals and hold you accountable. This helps us to become more intentional. Victory is accomplished through community and intentional spirituality.

C—Core Values

"As a man thinketh in his heart, so is he..."
(Proverbs 23:7, KJV)

In order to have experiential victory, believers must assess their personal core values. A core value can be defined as those boundaries a person refuses to cross because crossing those boundaries violates who God has created them to be and what God has called them to do.

I remember talking with a friend one time who told me that his neighbor said he could splice his satellite cable and run free cable to his house for him. My friend declined. I will never forget him saying, "Integrity is a core value of mine." Core values deal more with what we deem as valuable, not just what we believe. I was in a class at Southwestern Christian University where Dr. Garnet Pike was discussing core values. He had us write down all our core values. There were some dear brothers in the back that did not understand the concept of core values. They were "good ole denominational boys" and stated that their core values were the fourteen articles of faith of our denomination. Dr. Pike challenged them to step outside the box. He said, "What attitudes and actions do you hold dear and will not bend on?" That question changed their perspective greatly.

People who walk away from sin and bondage do so because they value righteous living. Someone who is trapped in pornography walks away because he or she values purity more than impurity. We have four gospel accounts of Jesus' life. From them, we can tell what Jesus did and did not value. His actions were a direct product of what He valued. Jesus said this in the Gospel of Matthew, "When you find a man's treasure, you will also find his heart." (Matthew 6:21, *paraphrased*). Take time to assess your "treasures."

Take time to write down your core values. What things in life will you not bend on? What things should you not bend on? Here are some examples of my core values: integrity, servant leadership, excellence, Spirit-empowered life, prayer, Bible study, and life-long learning. These values shape me and help to direct me. When I get out of line my core values get me back on the mark.

T—Training the Mind

> *Therefore gird up the loins of your mind, be sober, and rest your hope fully upon the grace that is to be brought to you at the revelation of Jesus Christ; as obedient children, not conforming yourselves to the former lusts, as in your ignorance (1 Peter 1:13-14, NKJV).*

The greatest battle that a believer will fight is the battle of the mind. The mind is the seat where thought and action are linked. Our minds can be great instruments for the Kingdom of God or they can be the greatest enemy in our lives. The way we perceive reality and the way we have experienced reality all enters through the vessel of the mind. We are products of our inner thought life. If we are to be the Kingdom generation and walk in the victory that heaven has already won for us, we must train our minds. Listen to this commentary:

> Gird up the loins. Christ's own words (Luke 12:35): an image from the Israelites eating the Passover with the loose outer robe girded up about the waist with a girdle, as for a journey. Workmen, pilgrims, runners, wrestlers, warriors (all types of the Christian), so gird themselves up, both to prevent the garment impeding motion, and to brace up the body for action. The believer is to have his mind collected, and always ready for Christ's coming. Sobriety—i.e., self-restraint, lest one be overcome by the allurements of the world and sense, and enduring waiting hope for Christ's revelation, are the true 'girding up the loins of the mind.'[14]

As you see, the writer of this commentary associates "girding up the loins of our minds" as Christ's second coming. Let's apply this to today. You are on a journey. As the Israelites had to prepare their garments for the journey, we must do the same with our minds.

Training our minds is not easy. As thoughts pass through and assumptions come, we must be able to reject those thoughts that slow down and impede our journey. Thoughts produce emotion. There are certain emotions that help us and there are certain emotions that hinder us. Assess your thoughts by saying, "What emotion is this thought producing and why am I thinking about it?"

I recently had a conversation about this with a dear friend of mine. His pastor shared a story one Sunday that relates to this subject. One of the routines that a Navy Seal has to go through in order to move forward is to be dropped into freezing water. People do not die from shock. People who are dropped in freezing water die from inhaling water. This routine is to teach them to train their mind to not react to the freezing water. Our lives should be the same way. We should train our minds not to react to sin when we are confronted with it.

O—Occasional Disciplines vs. Daily Disciplines

"I affirm, by the boasting in you which I have in Christ Jesus our Lord, I die daily" (1 Corinthians 15:31, NKJV).

Common men occasionally do what uncommon men do daily. John Maxwell calls this the *law of process*. The law states: "You don't become a leader in a day, but it is what you do day by day."[15] Any athlete who trains for an event has a rigorous daily routine. The athlete trains and works hard to get ready for the event on a daily basis. Imagine what would happen if an athlete just showed up the day before and told the coach he would just cram in workouts all day? The athlete would not be successful. One of the keys to victory is maintaining a daily routine or spiritual work out. You must take time to do the small things every day. Some Christians have the "all or nothing" spiritual philosophy. They think that if they cannot pray an hour a day and read a book of the Bible they are failing God and should just wait until they can. It is amazing what a couple of chapters in the Word and 15 minutes in prayer will do for a person. When walking in the experience of victory remember to obey the law of process. Do the small things each day that lead up to the big things.

R—Rock of Revelation

"...and on this rock I will build My church, and the gates of Hades shall not prevail against it" (Matthew 16:18, NKJV).

I have heard many sermons on this Scripture. Scholars often debate what Jesus meant by "on this rock." I want to open up an idea to you. Simon had the revelation that Jesus was God's Son—the Messiah. Jesus responded by making the "on this rock" statement. Jesus Christ had never been called "the Christ" at this point, and Simon had never been called Peter. Before this, his name was Simon which meant "reed." A reed is a plant that is easily blown by the wind. Jesus did not call him Simon, but Peter, which means rock. A rock is solid and cannot be moved. In essence, Jesus was saying, "Since you have a revelation of who I am, I can give you a revelation of who you are." Jesus said, "On this rock..." We were meant to live by the revelation of who God is.

Y—Your Victory is Linked to the Body

> *For as the body is one and has many members, but all the members of that one body, being many, are one body, so also is Christ. For by one Spirit we were all baptized into one body—whether Jews or Greeks, whether slaves or free—and have all been made to drink into one Spirit. For in fact the body is not one member but many (1 Corinthians 12:12-14, NKJV).*

When God sees you, He does not see only you, He sees the Body of Christ. In America we have become individualistic in our lives. One of the famous sayings of Americans is, "I gotta look out for #1." This has spilled over to our Christian outlook on life, also. We do not understand the concept that we are joined together with each other. If one person hurts or is weak, we are all weak.

When Joshua was lying on his face crying before the Lord he was told to get up and deal with the sin. The Lord said, "...all of Israel has sinned." It was only one man, but even then God viewed them as a whole. If our brother or sister does not live up to his or her ability, how much will that cost us? It will cost us a lot.

CONCLUDING THOUGHTS

One of God's names that He has revealed is *Jehovah Nissi*. Moses used this name for the Israelite's defeat of the Amalekites. This name means, "The Lord is My Banner." Literally, it means that the Lord is the One who sets us up on high with victory. As you are praying this week, take time to acknowledge God as *Jehovah Nissi*. Acknowledge that your victory is already sure in Him.

God has given us positional victory. This should also translate into experiential victory. Jesus has secured the victory for us already. He has already defeated every foe and enemy. We must trust in this and believe it. As we come into a greater knowledge of who He is through prayer and reading the Scriptures, He is able to reveal who we are in Him.

End Notes:
[12] Verbrugge, Verlyn D. *New International Dictionary of New Testament Theology*. Grand Rapids: Zondervan, 2000. Print.
[13] Verbrugge, Verlyn D. *New International Dictionary of New Testament Theology*. Grand Rapids: Zondervan, 2000. Print.
[14] *Jamieson, Fausset, and Brown Commentary*, Electronic Database. Copyright © 1997, 2003 by Biblesoft, Inc.
[15] Maxwell, John. *21 Irrefutable Laws of Leadership*. Nashville: Thomas Nelson, 1997. Print.

REFLECTION GUIDE

Take some time to reflect on these questions:

What is one element you read from this chapter that challenged you? Why?

What do you need to change in your thinking to apply the principles from this chapter?

What did you have the most trouble receiving because of previous teachings? Why?

What did you like the most about this chapter? Why?

CHAPTER 7

INFUSED WITH CREATIVITY

"'I am the Alpha and the Omega,' says the Lord God, 'who is, and who was, and who is to come, the Almighty.'" (Revelation 1:8)

In the beginning God created the heavens and the earth. Now the earth was formless and empty, darkness was over the surface of the deep, and the Spirit of God was hovering over the waters. And God said, "Let there be light," and there was light. God saw that the light was good, and he separated the light from the darkness. God called the light "day," and the darkness he called "night." And there was evening, and there was morning—the first day (Genesis 1:1-5).

LEFT BEHIND CULTURALLY

As I mentioned earlier, Jerry B. Jenkins and Tim LaHaye wrote a Christian book series called ***Left Behind***. These books focus on the rapture and the people that were left here on earth afterwards. These books should be the motto for the church in today's world; we truly have been left behind. Ninety percent of churches are twenty to thirty years behind the culture. Americans have detached from church because the church seems like some weird social club that has disconnected from society.

One of the main reasons for the "church lag" in this generation is that the church has separated itself from creative people. Only in the last fifteen years has dance, video, and art been widely accepted as actual ministry. We have seen a great explosion since that time, but the church still has to stand before the mirror of truth and realize their greatest asset in reaching this generation: creativity locked up in creative people.

GOD IS CREATIVE

Creativity and innovation are two of our core values in the church I lead. We wanted innovation to be one of the values we live and die by. Why? From our observation, it is because the church lacks so much creativity.

The first time we are introduced in Scripture to God, He is creating. Genesis chapter 1 deals with creation. God was creating something that had never been created before. He was taking something useless, the earth, and making it beautiful and useful for His greatest creation, people. God enjoyed creating and called it good. God is a creative person. God is the great artist. It is interesting that the first miracle Jesus did was changing the water into wine at a wedding: "This, the first of his miraculous signs, Jesus performed at Cana in Galilee. He thus revealed his glory, and his disciples put their faith in him" (John 2:11).

Every miracle that Jesus performed was also meant to be a lesson teaching about His deity. This miracle happened to teach that He is the Creator. God created the heavens and the earth by speaking. What did He speak? He used words. We are told in John chapter one that Jesus is the Word. We are also told throughout the New Testament that the world was created through Him and by Him. How did this happen? God created the heavens and earth through the Word. So when Jesus came on the scene we see Him creating something; Jesus changed the water into wine. Water was a normal substance. Wine was a substance that was used in celebratory situations. This creation was with existing materials. Jesus took an ordinary and bland substance and made it into a substance used for celebrating. This is what creative people do for the Body of Christ. Creative people take ordinary and bland church activities and make them extraordinary. I think we can all agree that we have been too bland in our church services.

Jesus was also creative in His style of teaching. He not only used Old Testament Scriptures to explain what God was doing; He used stories and real life situations to explain the Scriptures. Jesus used parables. There are many different descriptions of parables, but one of my favorite descriptions is "an earthly story with a heavenly meaning."[16] Jesus told stories in the language of that day that could explain to the people what God was saying. He painted captivating stories. People followed Christ for days without eating because they were so hungry to hear His truth. Jesus made truth colorful.

BEING SPIRIT-FILLED IS BEING CREATIVE

The first time that the Spirit of the Lord is mentioned filling someone in Scripture is to empower them to build and create. Read Exodus 35:30-35.

> *Then Moses said to the Israelites, "See, the LORD has chosen Bezalel son of Uri, the son of Hur, of the tribe of Judah, <u>and he has filled him with the Spirit of God, with skill, ability and knowledge in all kinds of crafts—to make artistic designs for work in gold, silver and bronze</u>, to cut and set stones, to work in wood and to engage in all kinds of artistic craftsmanship. And he has given both him and Oholiab son of Ahisamach, of the tribe of Dan, the ability to teach others. He has filled them with skill to do all*

kinds of work as craftsmen, designers, embroiderers in blue, purple and scarlet yarn and fine linen, and weavers—all of them master craftsmen and designers."

The church has many activities for those young people who like sports. There are sports recreation teams and church sports leagues. Churches spend millions of dollars a year for facilities to house these activities. Listen, I LOVE SPORTS! I was the creative guy growing up who loved sports. I loved art, as well. I didn't draw forests, though; I drew athletes. But in the modern day church it is the creative person who is left out. They are often the outcasts and the misunderstood. They are usually the teens who like their hair dyed and fingernails painted. They are also usually left to video games and reading sci-fi books. You can find creative "left outs" playing demonic video games and card games with other people like them. The church has to recognize that their greatest assets are creative people. Today, church leaders also have to recognize that the Spirit of God can rest on and use these people mightily for Him. Please don't look for them to come in to the church with suits and ties or a polo shirt. Please don't ask them to play in the church softball league. They will be interested in acting, dancing, singing, and drawing.

If this generation is to see heaven invade earth, we must value creativity in our churches. My good friend Brett Cooper's mission for 20/20 Youth Ministries is: "Guiding Creative Teenagers to Their Destiny in Jesus Christ." He did not reach the high school sports teams. His students played in the band, excelled in video games, and danced. They were musicians and artists.

A lot of today's churches lack an element of the Spirit of God. They do church the same way they have always done it. They are taught that creativity is great for the world, but it should not be used in church. It is very important for churches to note that the first time the Spirit of God is mentioned to "fill" someone was dealing with creativity in building the temple. I believe there are extremely creative people who God strongly desires to use in the church, but the church doesn't recognize their gifts as important. Most of those people find other places to use their creativity.

GOD CREATES, BUT SATAN IMITATES

God is the original author and creator. He is the creator of everything original. Satan cannot create anything original on his own; he imitates and perverts everything God creates. God created men and the earth, but satan through sin perverted them. There was a curse placed on the earth. After Genesis chapter three, the earth is referred to as, "the world." This Greek word *kosmos* is used in the New Testament to describe the system satan put in place to draw men to himself. Satan perverted what God created as good.

Movies and music are the primary teaching tools of our society. Sadly, the enemy has taken these tools and put in place, a worldly system which is educating our society. As a result of satan's worldly system, the church has labeled all movies as bad and "of the devil." God is the original movie producer. John Eldridge wrote a great book entitled ***Epic: The Story God is Telling*** . In this book, the author shares that the Bible is the book where all movies and stories are derived. There is perfect harmony, the harmony is disrupted by a villain, the villain captures the princess, and the hero rescues the princess back.[17] In today's Christian world, if a movie does not talk about Jesus every second, it is not "holy." A lot of the church does not understand the power of stories and how they shape values which in turn shape our lives. The generation is here which will make movies that will not only rival the genius of Steven Spielberg, but do greater things on God's behalf.

THE EXPRESSION OF THE CREATIVE PERSON

Creative people think and express themselves differently from others. It is important to know what, why, and how they think. There is unlimited potential which has not been tapped into because the church has failed to understand creative people. Imagine all the dance, drama, movies, video clips, and songs that have yet to be created! Let's take a look at the breakdown of the creative person.

1. Prolific: Creative People Generate Ideas.

The creative person is a person of unique ideas. They are always thinking of a more creative way to do something. When placed in a group of people, they can often push the status quo and desire change to traditional methods. Creative people bore easily and need an environment where they can bring change.

There are anchors, founders, builders, and creators in a church. The reason the modern church has not seen a great push is that the traditional church is full of anchors, founders, and a few builders. **Anchors** are those who have been there and are never leaving. **Founders** are foundation setters which provide the foundation for a church. **Builders** are those who are helping grow ministries and do most of the work. The new generational church that we deem as the emerging church is primarily built upon builders and creators; however there is a gap here. I believe the reason is because the traditional church feels threatened by the creator's innovative ideas that challenge the methods to which they have grown accustomed. The traditionalists attack the ideas of the creator which are the creator's most prized possession. The creator in turn leaves the church to find a group of other creators who will listen to their ideas.

2. Values: They Highly Value Their Ideas.

When the creative person's ideas are rejected they feel rejected. I operate as a creator and builder. I was taught by mentors to understand what an idea is and what an ideal is. It is important to validate the creative person's idea. Let them know that the idea is worth investigating, but you always need a backdrop or objective standard by which to evaluate it. A creative person can get lost in the search for the most creative way to solve a problem. However, they must lay their ideas against the vision of the church or the task at hand.

One of my staff members, Jim, is an extremely creative individual. It is a great joy working with him because he is always looking for a more creative model or way to do things. When we attended college together Jim was my associate in student ministry. During class, he would give me pages and pages of notes of ideas for the ministry. At first, I tried to figure out how these ideas could work so that I did not hurt his feelings by rejecting his ideas. I began to sit down with him and say, "Jim, is this just a random idea or can it fit with our vision and mission in this season?" After that, Jim began to filter his ideas by asking, "Is this an idea or an ideal?" Once he understood this, each idea he presented was powerful and focused.

3. Motivation: The Creative Person Needs Motivating.

The creator in your life, whether that is you or someone else, must be motivated to release his or her gifts in ministry. Creative people need creative environments; they need safe places to practice ideas. They need to be able to create and see the creation fall apart. Take an artist, for example. The artist needs a study where they can start with a blank pad and have the freedom to mess up in order to make the masterpiece.

It is important to find ministries and positions for creative people to attempt their ideas. They will want to initiate new things. Put them in places where you need creativity and give them permission to go after it. If you lock them into a position where their job is to maintain that ministry, they will shrink up and die. We allow our Community Groups not only to teach what is on their hearts, but they also choose a creative way to connect with the community each semester.

4. Wisdom: Truths the Creative Person Needs to Grasp Personally.

If you are a creative person and this describes you, take a few minutes to read this and evaluate yourself. Take time to be objective. Ideas are a dime a dozen. Digging for great ideas is like digging for gold. You have to dig through a lot of dirt to get to gold. You will have to go through a lot of "dirt" ideas to get to the golden ones.

Realize that the most creative way is not the best way. Learn to take your ideas and make them the team's idea. Your creative idea may only be part of the solution to the problem. The biggest obstacle to overcome is not to get defensive when your idea is refused. You may be in a season where you must learn from everyone else and not try to teach them through your ideas. This is the hardest truth to swallow. I can see when creative people on my team lose heart because their ideas are not being used. The question we must ask ourselves is, "Was my idea the best way for the team or just my way?"

THE EXPRESSION OF A CREATIVE CHURCH

All churches must have an element of creativity in them. As stated earlier, if God is the Creator of mankind and we have His image, then we must be creative. It is a shame to see a church that chooses to communicate the gospel with little creativity. I believe God gets excited when we ask for innovative ways to tell His story. If we are going to see heaven invade earth with the glory of God, creativity must be present. The creative church must look for new ways to communicate, relate, and develop people. The church can develop creativity and here are a few ways they can work at it:

1. Creative Communication.

One problem that churches face is how to bridge the generational gap. I was recently talking with an elderly retired Baptist minister and his wife. We were attending the service of a new church plant that had left the traditional model. The elderly couple did not really enjoy the church, so I took time to interview them. We talked about their history. They did not have TVs until they were in college. The radio was primarily used to listen to radio dramas. Music was not a big part of their life growing up or their church life.

Today, we can sing for thirty or forty-five minutes, but an older generation cannot do that. That is not their culture. The one element that did bind us together was TV. They enjoyed the same shows my wife and I do. They also talked about the church they regularly attend. One of the attractions at this church plant was that they used videos that mirrored the sermons the pastor was preaching. They were amazed by them, and they enjoyed them. That church was able to tap into a creative way of communicating the gospel to their people. Creative communication bridged the generation gap for them.

If your church service looks the same month after month with the style, structure, and physical setup that has always been used, you have lost that creative element. Strive to use media, stage decoration, thematic elements, and live dramas to speak about your topic. I love props. We plan our series out far enough in advance where we can incorporate props. I have used wigs, axes, shovels, and even a RUBIK'S CUBE®. Communicate with creative excellence.

2. Creative Relational Atmospheres.

Only in the last fifteen years has the church really tried to create authentic relationships between its members. Churches have relied upon their small size or their Sunday school classes to foster this. The world has become more relational with the explosion of companies such as Starbucks®. The world is seeking more authentic relationships; they desire to know and be known. The church has lost this dynamic.

Sure, small groups, cell groups, life groups, hot groups, or "whatever" groups, have been great at fostering this over the last 15 years. However, the truth of the matter is that we will have to develop even more creative atmospheres in order to continue to develop authentic relationships inside the church. It is important to create environments where people can learn to care about each other.

The church crucifies the "unlovable." Our love is often limited; it is only for those who are just like us. If the world is going to hunger after the gospel, they have to see authentic relationships. As an individual, what are you doing to foster authentic relationships? What is your church doing that it has never done to foster these types of relationships?

3. Creative Development of Leaders.

I have a friend who has caught the "life coaching model." This model leads with questions to pull potential out of the people being coached. He is fired up. You cannot go through one conversation without him bringing this up as the solution to all problems. Life coaching is a great model for pulling potential out of people and seeing their lives changed. The truth of the matter is that life coaching is the most creative model of personally developing people at this point or season in history. It deals with them discovering what they are uniquely called by God to accomplish. The moment someone finds a more creative and successful way, life coaching will be on the back burner. Churches must continually find more creative ways of developing people. We have used Sunday service and Wednesday service as our only model long enough. It is time to explore and push the status quo to find out the most fruitful way of releasing destiny inside of people. This can only happen in a small group atmosphere and through one-on-one development.

As I stated in my last book ***Taking the Next Step: Seven Principles for Leading the Emerging Church,*** we need to use innovative ways to develop a leadership culture. This means that we will have to find new ways to state old principles. For leadership development, we use ***Habitudes: Images that Form Leadership Habits & Attitudes*** by Tim Elmore[18]. If you have never used or read these, please order the set for your leadership training; through the use of images, leadership habits, and attitudes are illustrated. Find ways to creatively develop your principle. How will you develop people this year? What creative methods will be used?

CONCLUDING THOUGHTS

It is time for the church to realize that we need to hunger for creativity. God is THE Creator, so we must be creative. It took seven days to complete the creation of the earth. For the church to be complete, there must be a return to creativity. What has yet to be done? What solutions to the biggest problems have not been brought about yet? There are solutions to problems that God is waiting to reveal to you. All creative solutions come from questions that probe deeper. They ask, "Is there a better way to do this?"

Listen to this: during periods of great change, answers don't last very long, but a question is worth a lot. The word *question* is derived from the Latin *quaerere* (to seek), which has the same root as the word *quest*. A creative life is a continued quest where good questions are useful guides. We have found that the most useful questions are open-ended; they allow a fresh, unanticipated answer to reveal itself. These are the kinds of questions children aren't afraid to ask. They seem naive at first, but think how different our lives would be if certain questions of wonder were never asked. Jon Collins of Stanford's Graduate School of Business has compiled the following list of questions of wonder:

- Albert Einstein: What would a light wave look like to someone keeping pace with it?
- Bill Bowerman (inventor of Nike shoes): What happens if I pour rubber into my waffle iron?
- Fred Smith (founder of Federal Express): Why can't there be reliable overnight mail service?
- Godfrey Hounsfield (inventor of the CAT scanner): Why can't we see in three dimensions of what is inside a human body without cutting it open?
- Masaru Ibuka (honorary chairman, Sony): Why don't we remove the recording function and speakers and put headphones in the recorder? (Result: the Sony Walkman.)

Many of these questions were deemed ridiculous at first. Other shoe companies thought Bowerman's waffle shoe was a really stupid idea. Godfrey Hounsfield was told the CAT scanner was impractical. Masaru Ibuka got comments like, "A recorder with no speaker and no recorder—are you crazy?" Fred Smith proposed the idea of Federal Express in a paper at Yale and got a C."[19]

End Notes:

[16] Towns, Elmer. "New Testament Studies." DVD Online Class Liberty University. Liberty University, Lynchburg, VA. Tuesday Aug. 2003. Lecture.

[17] Eldredge, John. *Epic.* Nashville, TN: Thomas Nelson. 2004.

[18] Elmore, Tim. *Habitudes: Images That Form Leadership Habits & Attitudes.* Atlanta, GA: Growing Leaders, 2004. Print.

[19] Bits & Pieces, April 29, 1993, pp. 5-7.

REFLECTION GUIDE

Take some time to reflect on these questions:

What is one element you read from this chapter that challenged you? Why?

What do you need to change in your thinking to apply the principles from this chapter?

What did you have the most trouble receiving because of previous teachings? Why?

What did you like the most about this chapter? Why?

CHAPTER 8

INFUSED WITH AUTHORITY

Then I heard a loud voice in heaven say: "Now have come the salvation and the power and the kingdom of our God, and the authority of his Christ. For the accuser of our brothers, who accuses them before our God day and night, has been hurled down.

They overcame him by the blood of the Lamb and by the word of their testimony; they did not love their lives so much as to shrink from death. Therefore rejoice, you heavens and you who dwell in them! But woe to the earth and the sea, because the devil has gone down to you! He is filled with fury, because he knows that his time is short." (Revelation 12:10-12).

Then Jesus came to them and said, "All authority in heaven and on earth has been given to me. Therefore go and make disciples of all nations, baptizing them in the name of the Father and of the Son and of the Holy Spirit, and teaching them to obey everything I have commanded you. And surely I am with you always, to the very end of the age" (Matthew 28:18-20).

AUTHORITY VS. POWER

Imagine this: There are two huge men fighting in a ring. One can bench press 500 pounds while the other one can squat 500 pounds. They are powerful; they can take anyone down. As they begin to wrestle they are slamming, kicking, and punching. But at one juncture of the match, a small man who cannot bench or squat anywhere near that much steps in and tells these large men what to do. Here is the funny thing—they listen! He is wearing a white and black striped shirt and weighs about 120 pounds. This man is the referee and he has something that these other men do not have: authority. The referee has the legal authority to tell them what to do. The wrestlers are physically more powerful, but they have to listen to the man with the authority.

The struggle of the universe is not for power, but for authority. Power is the strength to perform, but authority is the legal right to tell power what to do. This illustration can be clearly seen in football. It is great when two huge linemen get in a tussle where they are pushing, grabbing face masks, and yelling. Then, the referee steps in and throws a flag, and these two men have to listen to his authority.

These two words are also seen in the New Testament. The word "power" comes from the Greek word *dynamis* (doo-na-mis), and the word "authority" comes from the Greek word *eksousia* (eksoo-see-ah)[20]. "Authority" is used sixty-seven times in the New Testament, usually in conjunction with Jesus' ministry.

The most familiar verse, but most misunderstood, is in Matthew 28:18-19 where Jesus tells His disciples, "All authority in heaven and on earth has been given to me. Therefore go..." (NIV). The King James Version translates this word *power*, but further study finds that a more accurate translation would be "authority." Power is much different from authority. *Eksousia* literally means, "delegated influence, or the power of government." *Dynamis* literally means, "strength, ability, or might." The Lord gave His disciples authority in the earth, and then He tells us to go use it. In Acts 1:8, Jesus tells the disciples when they will receive this power, "You will receive power when the Holy Ghost has come upon you" (KJV).

Satan has power. If you do not believe that, just look at the world today. The reason he has so much power is because he has not yet had to submit to authority. I heard one friend say, "The devil has power, but we have more power." That is a noble, but ignorant statement. We do have power, but the greater truth is that we have God's authority. God Himself has delegated His authority to His followers; He desires that we rule earth with His authority. Traditional conservative people hate this teaching. They often teach that the devil is going to beat us up until Jesus comes back. The great news is that we have authority to throw the flag and tell him that he will not destroy our generation.

KINGDOM AUTHORITY

When we are born again, we become citizens of heaven. As citizens, we have rights to the Kingdom. We do not have to wait for the rapture or for the millennial Kingdom to walk in these rights and privileges. He has in fact given us Kingdom authority now.

The early Christians did not fight the government with petitions and radio shows, and they lived in a much more corrupt government society than we do today. Their persecution was much stronger than ours, but the funny thing is that the gospel was being spread more effectively. There was an outbreak of revival so strong that it was scaring the leaders of the countries being affected by it. The early Christians operated in Kingdom authority. They had influence by showing the world something it had never seen before. The church today cannot be accused of failing to recycle; that is all the church does. It recycles formulas for "successful" ministry. The church is a copycat society that is intoxicated with the idea of being successful. In the midst of this, we have lost the passion for being significant and unique. We have lost the passion for those far from God. We have lost the idea of being infused and invading our world with the love of God.

EVERY CHRISTIAN IS A MINISTER

Ministry is more than just working on staff at a church. Ministry is where God has called us to invest our lives; it is service to the Most High. The church assigns any Christian who is on fire for God to "church ministry." Any young Christian who does not have a certain revival experience is relegated to another educational pursuit. Our church traditions fail us in not emphasizing that we are all ministers wherever we are; ministry must extend outside the four walls of the church building.

There is a breakdown in American Christian churches. The church in America has radio broadcasts, petitions, and picket lines to try to stop certain groups. Some preachers preach "anti-sermons" which are against everything like a kid spitting spitballs across a classroom. There is a strategy the enemy is using that the church has not yet grasped; satan is placing his people in areas of authority to influence society. They may be loud minority groups that are opposed to the gospel, but they are rising in ranks of authority to make decisions for the whole of our country.

THE 7 MOUNTAIN STRATEGY

I want to introduce to you the idea of the Seven Mountain Strategy. This may be your first time reading about this or you may have been exposed to this idea previously. If the church is going to see Kingdom authority established in the earth, it must understand how to influence culture. That is what this strategy is all about. Bill Bright and Loren Cunningham were two people who brought this idea to the forefront. Landa Cope tells this story in her book entitled, ***The Old Testament Template***.[21] This is a great book for study on the seven mountains. Loren and Bill were planning on having a lunch meeting one day. The night before, both of them had a dream about mountains and the authority in these mountains. They did not know that the other one had this dream. When they met for lunch both kept trying to share their dream from the night before! We will look at the essence of what they dreamed.

Some break this down into twelve mountains, and some have ten. Here, we are going to break everything down into seven major mountains. There are seven structures in which our world operates; we will call these structures mountains. Each mountain is a power structure where influence is released. There is the mountain of religion, education, business, government, arts and entertainment, media, and family. The enemy taught the church that it does not need to strive to be the leader of these structures. We are taught that this is selfish ambition, and we should spend more time working for the growth of the local church.

Dr. Lance Wallnau gives a great illustration of this from one of his conferences[22] where he was teaching on this subject in Korea. He was asked how many Fortune 500 business leaders were in the audience. There were none; Korea has always been behind in this area. As he was teaching, a man stood up and began to weep. The man told him that he had the desire to be the president of his country. He was taught through the church that "spiritual" Christians help build the church. He assumed that it was just a passing selfish ambition. He repented and wept before the large audience. As he was standing and weeping, business leaders in his country came around him and started praying. After the prayer time, one business leader told him that if the man would go back to school and have the proper training to run for the presidency, he would back him. One by one, Christian leaders in that country stood up and said the same thing. This man is undergoing the proper training at this time to be a candidate for presidency. What would happen if a true believer became president of that country? Of any country? Christians are called to reign in this life and operate in Kingdom authority in every area.

THE SEVEN MOUNTAINS

Let's take a walk through the seven mountains:

1. Religion: He is Lord of lords and God of gods.

The mountain of religion is one for those who are called into full-time clerical ministry. Their job is to advance their religion and find ways of creatively sharing their beliefs to the world. As Christians, we know that we do worship the One True God, but we face a society that puts us in one pot with all other religions. I have been primarily called to the mountain of religion. My job is to gain influence and find creative ways to share the truths of the gospel. I must also focus on how to equip the ones in the congregation to take the mountain to which they have been called.

The Islamic faith is currently the fastest growing religion in the world. They are taking this mountain from Christians. Christianity must have leaders who are fearless. There are some pastors who view their ministry as a vocation, rather than a calling. There are professional preachers who seek reputation, wealth, and job security; however, we need pastors in America who hunger after the things of God to the point where they will risk money and position. When leaders lead with total abandonment toward the things of God the church will follow.

2. Education: He is the Great Teacher.

One of the favorite titles the disciples gave Jesus was Rabbi or Teacher. God can be seen throughout the Bible as a God who is interested in educating His people. Proverbs says that wisdom was in the beginning with God when He created the heavens and the earth. The book of Proverbs alone shows us that God is not interested in people who only serve Him, but in helping His people to be people of wisdom, knowledge, and understanding. Jesus was trained under the rabbis of His day; during Jesus' time, it was customary for boys to receive an education. The gospels show us that Jesus learned fast! At twelve years of age, He was bringing amazing questions to the teachers of the law.

Moses was instructed to teach the people of Israel about all areas of life. However, Moses did not do Bible studies all day, he taught the people what it meant to live sanitary lives, increase in wealth, operate in proper relationships, and worship God properly. The teachers in our American school system will shape and direct this country's future. They are able to instill godly values or ungodly values. They are able to show compassion and help children, or they can be there for a paycheck and operate merely as a hireling. There was a tremendous amount of responsibility on Moses, as he had to disciple or teach an entire nation the values of God.

3. Business: He is *Jehovah Jireh*, our Provider.

Contrary to popular belief, God is interested in money. Many churches are shying away from the teachings of finance and increase, but the Bible has a lot to say about it. There are many Scriptures that address this subject, but let's look at one in particular: "But the wealth of the sinner is stored up for the righteous" (Proverbs 13:22, NKJV). I have heard this so many times, but I never sat down and pondered on this verse. How does this happen? Does this mean that sinners will send miracle checks to me? That has happened to people before, but I believe the main way we will see this is through the mountain of business. Commerce and trade are ways in which the wealth of the sinner or wicked will be transferred into the account of the righteous. God's plan is much bigger than miracle checks in the mail. God is using business leaders to invade corporate structures and share the gospel of Christ through a divine competency that the world has not yet seen. When we can produce results superior to the world's results, we will get the world's attention.

We must not ask for favor over our businesses to cover up incompetence, but we must begin to ask for God's favor so we can have increase in finance and influence in order for the gospel of Christ to go forth. The coming revival will not be televised at a church, but the revival that will truly shake our land will happen in the marketplace and in the streets. Jesus did 90% of his miracles in the marketplace. We continue to ask God to do something He never planned to do: bring earth shaking revival through a church service. Many major revivals of the past happened through business owners and workers getting together and praying.

4. Arts and Entertainment: He is the Potter and Creator.

As stated in the chapter on creativity, God is creative. All ideas and creations originated at some point in Him. God is an artist, sculptor, builder, and singer. Jesus even entertained guests at the wedding in Cana of Galilee. The Bible describes God as all of these. This mountain may be the true educator of the people of our generation. Where do most people learn attitudes, behaviors, language, and interaction with others? They learn through movies, music, and entertainment. I watch young men walk down the street with angry looks on their faces while they are quoting and singing music lyrics of hate which are being taught by the arts and entertainment industry. For years, the church has told us that movies and non-church music is bad. So the church listened and removed itself from that realm. As movies and music have invaded our culture, we have seen a shift away from Christianity. This is truly Babylon's education center. Young men and women are taught that purity is a joke. Adults are taught to take vengeance on those who wrong them. We are being taught to pull for bad guys. There needs to be more Christian actors who will infiltrate the ranks of Hollywood and share the gospel with people. We cannot hold the people of Hollywood to such a high standard if there are no Christians there to share the gospel.

5. Family: He is God our Father.

God is introduced in the New Testament as our Father, and we are His children. Christians are described as "sons" and "daughters." The family is the most basic building block of society. When the family breaks down, society breaks down. The enemy has done a great job of breaking down the family unit in America.

We are taught to have non-committed marriages. We are taught that same-sex marriage is normal and should be tolerated when the Bible does not condone it. In the Bible, we see that morals and the teachings of the Word are passed down through the family (Deuteronomy 28). If the parents are more childish than the children, then who teaches the children? Our breakdown of morality in America has stemmed from the breakdown of the family unit. We will continue to see a demonic attack on the foundation of the family unit as the time of Christ's return nears.

6. Media: He is the Word (Communication).

The media in America is another great teacher of the world's system that is currently run by satan. The majority of our television stations are run by liberals who teach from a filtered point of view. The way our country has been changed and is being changed is mainly through media. Christians are taught what to believe by CNN® and other news stations. Their liberal anchors hate Christianity and anything to do with it. When election time comes, they are the first to try and make a Christian candidate look ridiculous. These people are a minority, but they are claiming the mountain. Actors and TV show hosts are the pastors of this country. I hate to say it, but Oprah Winfrey and Ellen Degeneres are America's leading pastors (culture enforcers).

The church must begin to raise up people who can infiltrate these systems and promote the good news of Christ. We must encourage our young people to go into those systems and change them. The History Channel® is our nation's Sunday school teacher. They are teaching people what to believe about Jesus, Paul, Moses, and biblical miracles. Until we understand the enemy's strategy, he will continue to have the minority teach the majority on what they should believe about religion, politics, and the family.

7. Government: He is the Judge.

Supreme Court justices have been making up new laws instead of holding to justice in our country. They are the deciding factors when it comes to morality and absolute truth in America. Twelve justices (the minority) have claimed the mountain and are making decisions for the nation (the majority). Even if all of America did not want a decision to happen, these justices have the authority to change laws and allow the minority to speak forth.

Our God is the Righteous Judge. He is the One who stands for morality and righteousness. Instead of shooting spitballs from our little-heard radio stations and pulpits, we must encourage believers to run for government offices. We must stop trying to overthrow government decisions with petitions alone, and start supporting true Holy Ghost-filled candidates who will rule with righteousness; we must support police officers, judges, and lawyers who will help govern our nation with righteousness.

HOW TO INFILTRATE THE SYSTEM AND TAKE OVER A MOUNTAIN

LESSONS FROM JOSEPH

1. Revelation of the Call

In the early years of Joseph's life, he received a dream that God gave him. He had a dream that his destiny was to be a ruler. Joseph believed this because he told people about it with excitement. Many of us are living day-to-day without realizing that we have a divine call on our lives. Remember the call of God is not delegated to pulpit ministers; we are all ministers. Before we can infiltrate the system, we have to be awakened to the call. Whether you are a school teacher, mechanic, garbage collector, or pulpit minister, God has called you there to be able to share the values of the gospel and infiltrate that system.

2. Divine Competence in the Call

Joseph excelled wherever he went and in whatever he did. Whether in Potiphar's house or in jail, Joseph was excellent in what he did. He worked the hardest, had the best attitude, and produced the most results. Our biggest problem today is that Christians are usually the laziest workers, the most incompetent, and most unfaithful. They enjoy preaching, but they do not enjoy preaching by example.

We must have divine competence in the call. *Competence* literally means "being able to get the job done right." A competent person is someone the manager can count on. A competent person is someone who can produce superior results. Let me ask this question: if you have the God of the universe living inside of you, shouldn't you have an edge on the rest of your non-Christian peers in the workplace? Leaders listen to competent people. Do you arrive early and leave late? Do you have a great attitude that attracts others? When you are asked to do a job, do you waste time on the internet and talking to others?

3. Knowing the Spiritual Significance of Your Positioning

Joseph knew that at every level, he was positioned for God to use him. He also knew that God was teaching him and shaping him at every level. Joseph knew that the sovereign hand of God had allowed him to be in that circumstance. You may not like your job, and you may think God is punishing you, but you are wrong—dead wrong. God is trying to teach you and trying to teach others through you. Joseph knew he was positioned in the good times and bad times. As you walk into your place of business, allow yourself to say, "This is the day the Lord has made."

CONCLUDING THOUGHTS

God has given us authority and power. His Sovereign hand is on our lives. He desires that we see national change through reclaiming the seven mountains that we have lost. If we are going to see heaven brought to earth, we must have Holy Ghost-filled believers in every area of life infiltrating the system.

End Notes:
[20] Verbrugge, Verlyn D. *New International Dictionary of New Testament Theology*. Grand Rapids: Zondervan, 2000. Print.
[21] Cope, Landa. *An Introduction to the Old Testament Template: Rediscovering God's Principles for Discipling Nations*. 2nd ed. Seattle: YWAM, 2011. Print.
[22] Wallnau, Lance. "Discipling Nations." Marketplace Ministry. Conference Center, Atlanta. Thursday Sept. 2007.

REFLECTION GUIDE

Take some time to reflect on these questions:

What is one element you read from this chapter that challenged you? Why?

What do you need to change in your thinking to apply the principles from this chapter?

What did you have the most trouble receiving because of previous teachings? Why?

What did you like the most about this chapter? Why?

CHAPTER 9

SO WHAT?

CONCLUDING THOUGHTS AS YOU GO

I want to take the next few minutes and just share. I am stepping out of the author and writer phase at this point. Let's pretend we are sitting over a cup of coffee and this conversation came up. Let's pretend that for the last couple of hours we have discussed this book. As we are parting ways, I want to give you some lasting thoughts.

The point of this book is for you to look at your life objectively. Let's just stop thinking about how many times we go to church and what we give. What do you want your tombstone to say?

I ask you to wake up and know that God's desire is to see His Kingdom established on earth. He wants to infuse earth with the glory of heaven. He wants to see you walk in your fullest potential.

As you read this book, you may realize that you sincerely love God, but that you are going through the motions of life. You and your husband bought that home. Your car is almost paid off. You have filed for the 401K plan at work. You give to church. You even have your kids somewhat involved. That is great, but I think you just missed God's purpose for your life. How are you ushering in the presence of God Almighty into the earth today? Is your life really bathed with expectation of the things that the Almighty is going to do in your life on a daily basis? Do you know that you are a missionary on assignment from God and your neighborhood is your mission field?

Planet Earth is the mission field. Our assignment is in whatever we are currently involved. I pray for you, my friend, that you take what I have given you as a stepping stone to see heaven activated on earth.

ABOUT THE AUTHOR

DR. KEVIN BORDEAUX grew up in Turkey, North Carolina. After running from God while being consumed with drugs and alcohol, Kevin surrendered his life to Christ. He was delivered from addiction and immediately began working for the Lord. He started a Christian Punk Rock Band called, "The Combat Junkies" which toured from 1999-2003. Kevin played guitar, wrote songs and managed the band, but most importantly, he shared the gospel in some of the darkest places in the U.S.

In 2003, Kevin met his wife Dianna in Clinton, North Carolina. Afterwards, he accepted the call to church ministry and left for Emmanuel College in Franklin Springs, Georgia. Kevin and Dianna married in 2006, and they both graduated from Emmanuel College the next year. He completed his Bachelors of Arts in Christian Ministries with a focus in New Testament *Koine* Greek. Then he went on to finish his Masters of Ministry in Christian Leadership from Southwestern Christian University and earned his Doctoral Degree from Covenant Bible College and Seminary.

Kevin has served in every possible ministry role you can imagine. He has planted three churches, served as a youth, associate, and lead pastor, as well as been part of two church mergers. He is currently serving as lead pastor of Thrive Church in Richmond, Virginia and serves as the Evangelism Director of Redemption Ministries. In addition to speaking on a wide range of topics around the nation, Kevin coaches new church plant pastors, as well as revitalization projects.

Kevin and Dianna live in Richmond where Dianna works as a Physician Assistant. They have two dogs: Bailey and Ruby. You can find out more about Kevin and his work at Thrive Church at *www.ThriveChurch.me.*

ALSO AVAILABLE FROM KEVIN BORDEAUX

Taking the Next Step: Seven Principles for Leading the Emerging Church

With our society changing at a rapid pace, the culture of the church is changing, also. The essence of being a church leader has radically changed in the last decade. In order for a pastor to successfully lead a 21st century emerging church, Pastor Kevin has developed seven principles that will help them know the next step in leading the coming generations. This message will help you launch into your destiny for such a time as this.

The Seven Principles discussed are:

- The Principle of Self-Leadership
- The Principle of Vision
- The Principle of Corporate Leadership
- The Principle of Excellence
- The Principle of Strategic Planning
- The Principle of Corporate Sowing
- The Principle of Prayer

ISBN 978-142599-871-4
Paperback: 140 pages
Publisher: AuthorHouse
Retail: $12.99 USD

Available at your local bookstore or order online at www.Amazon.com or email ThriveChurchVA@gmail.com

Parsons Publishing House

Your Voice Your World™

Infuse—Activating Heaven on Earth by Dr. Kevin Bordeaux

This book will guide you in your understanding of how to have a living, dynamic relationship with God and then spread that relationship to the world. Jesus told us to pray, "On earth as it is in heaven." To do this, we must know what is happening in heaven. The Book of Revelation is not only a futuristic, apocalyptic account, but a glimpse into heaven. It is also a glimpse into how our lives can be funnels where the world can experience heaven daily through us.

ISBN: 978-1-60273-011-3 • 138 pages • $12.95 USD

Next Level: Raising the Standard of Grace by Robert Gay

In this book, Robert is sounding a trumpet call from heaven, engaging the reader to see the Ten Commandments afresh from the empowering view of God's Grace. Robert clearly and biblically explains how Grace empowers us to live godly, holy lives above sin. There is no limit to the success, prosperity, and blessings that will surround you when you apply these principles.

ISBN: 978-160273-042-7 • 216 pages • $14.95

Surviving the Challenges of Transition—Nuggets to Remember on the Way to Your Dream by Dr. Gerald Doggett

As an IPHC minister, Dr.Gerald Doggett exhorts the reader in his second book to not let their past dictate their future. He provides exciting nuggets which include: It's OK to Remain A Chair!, Your Dream Will Attract Favor & Warfare, God Restores Everything That Has Been Lost!, and Sometimes You Need to Have A Party!

ISBN: 978-1-60273-018-2 • 140 pages • $12.95 USD

Portrait of a Pastor's Heart—A Manual on Caring for the Sheep by Bishop Gerald Doggett

This book is a must for pastors, elders, students & laymen who want to learn how to care for the flock of God. Bishop Gerald Doggett paints a rare and intimate portrait covering TOPICS such as: Spirit of a Finisher, The Necessity of the Divine Call and A Beautiful Portrait of Preparation.

ISBN: 978-1-60273-001-4 • 140 pages • $12.95 USD

Setting the Course for Future Generations by Shane Huseby

God is a God of generations! The God of Abraham, Isaac and Jacob is the same God of Christians today and He is issuing a charge to today's families–today's fathers–to invest in and impart to this next generation of young people. In this exciting book, Shane Huseby takes a look at contemporary families and how we can answer God's charge.

ISBN: 978-1-60273-024-3 • 120 pages • $9.95 USD

Why Do I Do the Things I Do?—Understanding Personalities by Darrell Parsons

In this insightful book, Darrell Parsons identifies the four primary types of personalities and how they interact together. As you grow in understanding, you will gain the tools you need for developing successful relationships in all areas of your life.

ISBN: 978-1-60273-019-9 • 132 pages • $10.95 USD

Release Your Words—Impact Your World by Darrell Parsons

Your words can make a difference! God has placed treasures inside you; learn to release them to influence your world. In this book, Darrell Parsons challenges you to use your voice to impact the world around you today.

ISBN: 978-1-60273-000-7 • 140 pages • $9.95 USD

CAPTURING THE HEART OF GOD—Pleasing the Father in Everyday Life by Diane Parsons

God created man for His good pleasure. Make it your goal today to do those things which please God. This book contains practical tips on how to turn the face of God toward you and become His delight every day.

ISBN: 978-1-60273-008-3 • 128 pages • $10.95 USD

Available at your local bookstore or order online at www.Amazon.com